PRAISE FOR FIERCE AWAKENINGS

Fierce Awakenings is a journey that reaches into the heart of every woman, wherever she is on her spiral path. Through the telling of individual stories, this book lifts the vibration of all women moving through heartbreak, loss, grief, self-doubt, personal pivots, and professional reinvention. It energizes and empowers us to discover more of who we are, and invites us to embrace, embody, and raise the frequency of our consciousness, awareness, and present-moment experience.

— JERALYN GLASS, PROFESSOR, SOUND
HEALING PIONEER, AUTHOR, AND CREATOR
OF CRYSTAL CADENCE

Fierce Awakenings is a magnificent convergence of divine feminine energy that lovingly guides us to boldly step into our power and own our impact. The stories are profound – the lessons are priceless.

— DAVIDJI, AUTHOR OF *SACRED POWERS*

John,
May these stories inspire
your personal journey!
Much love,

Fierce awakenings are waiting to be claimed when women listen to their hearts...when they stop people-pleasing... when they question society's expectations... when they literally or figuratively burn away what no longer serves them. Being aware of these fierce awakenings and walking life's spiral path take courage and confidence. The women in this book show us how to discover just enough of both to keep taking the next step. They rest in the sacred pause, feel into what is true now, and, then with deep knowing and trust, rise up again. Each author invites us to be who we truly are without shame, guilt, or compromise. They remind us that we can say, "Yes. I am here, and I do matter."

— BERNADETTE PLEASANT, FOUNDER OF THE
EMOTIONAL INSTITUTE AND
TRANSFORMATIONAL PUBLIC SPEAKER

The *Fierce Awakenings* anthology is a symphony of women's voices, with each narrative echoing deeply with authenticity and raw emotion. These stories spiral—meandering into the depths of the self as they simultaneously spiral outward, capturing the intricate dance between internal exploration and the external world. The women you encounter within this book's pages are living, breathing testimonies of resilience.

— KATIE CURTIN, CREATIVE LIFE AND BOOK
COACH, FOUNDER OF THE ONLINE
CREATIVITY CAFE

The world desperately needs more fiercely awakened women —women with hearts brimming with compassion, minds ablaze with brilliance, and the courage to articulate the truth of their unique experiences. This illuminating book offers a kaleidoscope of perspectives, each author exploring new insights, profound understandings, and transformative awakenings. I passionately encourage everyone to dive into its pages and be captivated by the powerful wisdom it imparts.

— SCOTT W. MILLS, PH.D., EXECUTIVE COACH

As women, we are often steeped in *What's wrong with me!* This book tells us what's right with us. Wonderful gems of "moving inward and upward" remind me the work of self-discovery is never done. Each chapter helps peel the onion back on the many layers of our own life's adventure to be "voluntarily vulnerable and boldly brave."

— DONNA LUBRANO, PROFESSOR OF INTERNATIONAL BUSINESS AND VIRTUAL EXCHANGE/COIL EXPERT

I felt she had shined a light on my own life, reuniting me with pieces of myself which had long been thought of as flaws, now understanding they're part of the gifts I bring to my relationships and the world.

— NONI WHITE, ACTRESS AND SCREENWRITER

This is a simple and touching compilation of true stories from remarkably real women. These stories reveal to us that awakening is not some far off idea for women granted special powers and privilege. Rather, it is a way of living where we meet our lives from the fullness of our fear, our anger, our joy, and our courage to be available for life as it unfolds in and through us. *Fierce Awakenings* is an invitation for each of us to find magic in our mundane, beauty in our pain, and meaning through meeting the precious ingredients of our lives nakedly as ourselves.

— KATHERINE ZORENSKY, SHAMAN, AUTHOR
AND FOUNDER OF THE TECHNOLOGY OF LOVE

CALLING IN COURAGE AND CONFIDENCE
TO WALK LIFE'S SPIRAL PATH

"A JOURNEY THAT REACHES INTO THE
HEART OF EVERY WOMAN"
- JERALYN GLASS

Fierce
Awakenings

FIERCE AWAKENINGS

CALLING IN COURAGE AND CONFIDENCE TO WALK LIFE'S SPIRAL PATH

JENNIFER BALJKO   SHAWNA BURKHOLDER

NICOLE FABIAN   ROXANNA FIGUEROA   KATHY GATES

SARAH HOSKIN   ELLISON JAMES   APRIL LEE

JOSETTE MILLS   WENDY PETERMAN, PH.D.

SUSAN K. SMITH   JOANNA LYNN STEFFEL

CONTENTS

DEDICATION

This collaborative book is dedicated to all the women, everywhere, embracing their fierce awakenings and stepping forward with courage, confidence, and creative chutzpah. May our spiral paths intertwine, and may we walk onwards together in sisterhood.

With hands on our hearts, we extend gratitude to all of our mentors, guides, and teachers, alive and in spirit, who helped us see our own next steps as visionaries and way-makers. We are, in part, who we are now because of your grace, patience, and wisdom.

FOREWORD

BY SIERRA MELCHER

Can you hear me?

Somewhere along the way, I picked up a story about the *"right way"* to live life. Do you have a story like that?

The story I carried around with me for a long time had a lot of straight lines in it. A lot of destinations, and a lot of sharp edges and corners. I never really fit into that story.

For most of my growing up, and adulthood, I believed that meant something was wrong with *me*. I wasn't a straight line. I had soft curves where sharp edges were preferred. I worked to straighten out. To step in line and stay on the "right path."

It was exhausting.

Until I discovered something.

Life does not need to be a straight line. In fact, very few things, if anything in life actually contain straight lines:

- The moon is round and changes every night
- The seasons follow a cyclical and spiral path
- Nature and everything that we live in, on, and around abides by this cyclical spiraling rhythm

This was not an easy shift for me – to realize that the story I had lived by, regardless of how uncomfortable it was, was not a story that had space for me. It didn't really match with the world that I saw around me. But for years, I still managed to resist that realization and stay stuck because I held tight to what I thought I understood, what I believed was expected and required of me.

Likewise, I have this illusion that if I were lucky enough to get an awakening, it would be a blissful well-lit, cinematographic, joyous moment. But I've been doing this for a while. And I have never met a pretty realization. All awakenings are messy, by definition. It is part of what makes them beautiful.

Contained within are the stories of 12 women, all of whom share their ***fierce awakenings***, messy and glorious. Soften into it to discover new ways of being and break this dominant paradigm.

INTRODUCTION

One evening, in October 2021, during one of those in-between pandemic periods of confinement and freedom, the wind that sometimes whispers to me gave me a message:

"Bring them together. Let everyone see their gifts. Share their stories."

I stared out of the train window, watching the full moon shimmer on the vineyards, hoping I could ignore the cryptic message from who-knows-where that just fell into my heart.

"Bring who together, to do what?" I ventured telepathically, wondering what new invitation had inadvertently pulled into my already-full life.

"The women, of course."

Just as those words rose up, I glimpsed through the highlight reel of a vision I had many months earlier. During a powerful meditation offered by my mentor Jocelyn Star Feather, I had seen myself running through a sunlit forest with Goddesses Artemis and Lilith and hundreds of women beside me. We were the epitome of fierce, fun, and fantastic. Together, we arrived at a village, formed a huge circle dozens of rings wide, and the goddesses handed each of us our unique gifts. From this vision, I debuted the Fierce Awakened

Woman online conference in the spring of 2021 and was now planning the 2022 iteration.

Believing I was already fulfilling the dream and confused by the latest call, I sent out a follow-up question, directing it to the moon, "Can you please clarify, which women and in what way?"

"It's a book, Jenn. Do you see it?"

For many months after that, I didn't want to see it. I had hoped that the wind had caught the attention of the wrong person, that the task was meant for someone else. I doubted my ability to take on such a multifaceted project, to gather up and lead a group of women through a writing, editing, and publishing triathlon.

I cringed. I cowered. I contested Spirit's choice.

Then, I remembered.

Sierra Melcher, one of my first conference speakers, had started Red Thread Publishing. She and her team had created a platform where women came together in circle, opened their hearts, shared their stories, imparted their wisdom, and stood proudly with dauntless authority.

Knowing that I didn't have to do this alone gave me the courage and confidence I needed to finally say, "YES! Show me the women!"

Fierce Awakenings, the collaborative book you're holding now, is one step on my spiral path, the path that moves me both inwards and upwards towards my highest potential. It is also a leap forward for each of the 11 other women who have chosen to be voluntarily vulnerable and boldly brave in revealing their joys and sorrows, their soft spots and their grit. Likewise, this book may offer you, dear Reader, the nudge you've wished for, the boost of fierceness you've been seeking, so you, too, can live your wonder-filled life with joy and awe.

Influenced as much by Maureen Murdock's *The Heroine's Journey* and Jean Shinoda Bolen's *The Millionth Circle* as by the themes and archetypes represented in the Tarot and astrological zodiac houses, *Fierce Awakenings* takes us on a leisurely walk into the center of our own experiences and allows us to witness our constant evolution, accumulated choices, and continual becoming.

The essays you're about to read unfold the complexities that come in the healing of childhood wounds, abandonment, complacency, poverty, divorce, sickness, addiction, systemic injustice, misdirected expectations, identity dilemmas, imposter syndrome, and death.

Surely, too, you'll recognize the range of emotions and energy that spin from states of confusion, anger, grief, and resignation. And then, from those depths, you'll notice the pivotal moments that led to awareness, daringness, resilience, and love.

Each chapter is a signpost on the lifetime journey to authenticity, belonging, grace, integrity, and wholeness.

Each author offers a beacon to others walking life's spiral path, adding her light to the collective's expansive reach.

Each woman shares her gift, unique to her and yet universal to all women navigating the twists and turns of life with their own blend of courage, confidence, and creative chutzpah.

Fierce One, for a little while, lay down your backpack filled with life's woes and worries.

Come into a circle of sisterhood.

Wait for the wind to whisper to you the fierce awakening that always calls you back to the spiral path.

Take your next step. We'll walk with you.

With joy and wonder,
Jenn Baljko

THE SPIRAL PATH

SARAH HOSKIN

I was an experienced pilgrim.

I was clear and confident, at least until I arrived at Carn Lês Boel, an outcropping of rocks above the coastal cliffs west of Lands End. This was the beginning of the Mary Michael Pilgrims Way, a relatively new pilgrimage path that serpentines along the Michael Alignment across southern England from this most southwestern point in Cornwall all the way over to the east coast of England. My plan was to walk to Glastonbury Tor, the halfway mark, through the lands of my ancestors–Cornwall, the land of my father, and Somerset, the land of my mother–to find and reconnect with my roots.

Always a walker, I became aware of walking a sacred pilgrimage path when a used copy of Shirley MacLaine's *The Camino* fell into my hands. At that moment, I knew that someday I would walk the Camino de Santiago in Spain, and that walking a pilgrimage path would become my healing path, my way home to wholeness. Walking the Camino three times evolved into walking the Mary Michael Way in Great Britain.

Born in England and raised in the United States, I did not grow up around extended family. I missed knowing my grandparents and cousins. Even more, I did not know much about those who came before me, or the land they lived and died on.

I was both, but also neither, British or American. Over time, this translated into a split that deeply affected and informed me into my adult life, showing up in many ways…Diastasis Recti, a physical split in my abdominal muscles, widened over four pregnancies… low core strength…being told I had no core or center…looking outside of myself for cues and rules…a prevailing sense of not belonging or fitting in…a challenging disconnect with my mother…an unrootedness to place…and, most deeply, a separation from an embodied spiritual source. I was lonely and lost in the midst of my rich and full life. Healing the split became my focus, mantra and intention. Walking pilgrimages became my path to healing.

Now, for the first time, I was all alone on the pilgrimage path. There were no yellow Camino arrows to show me the way to go. No other pilgrims going the same direction. Just me, my gear, a compass, a map, and guidebooks, way out at the far end of this remote peninsula.

A warm breeze gently nudged me inland.

Leaving the coast behind me, I crossed a field of heather, passed through a wooden gate and came across Far Away Cottage, a lonely and isolated cottage, now a holiday rental.

I too felt far away. I was scared. What was I doing?

On a gravel road, I looked up and saw myself from thousands of feet up in the sky — a 53-year old woman, walking alone, far out on a wide open landscape, following a map, inspired by a crazy idea to heal a split and find my roots.

I doubled over in anguish. What was I thinking? How could I do this?

I slowly stood up and began to sing.

Kumbaya my Lord.

Kumbaya, my Lord, kumbaya!

Kumbaya, my Lord, kumbaya!

O Lord, kumbaya!

I took the next steps. I sang the verses I knew. I made up new ones. *Kumbaya* evolved into a chant that I made up as I walked,

Walking the Path of the Marys. Calming myself, I sang these words over and over.

I am walking the path of the Marys, of the Marys, of the Marys.
I am walking the path of the Marys.
Mother Mary. Mary Magdalene. Mary Salome. All the Marys.

I walked through a tiny village, greeted by the local geese, and passed a cricket green before veering left onto a smaller road. At the bottom of the hill, I crossed a stone bridge and turned left up a narrow lane that took me around another hill through a dilapidated stone farm. The guidebook said that there was an ancient well up ahead.

The air was fragrant with warm salty sea air and summer blossoms. I had found my stride and noticed that I was no longer nervous. The road descended into a shaded, cooler enclave of houses and stone walls. Ahead of me was a white gate. To my lower right was a barely visible slate marked The Well 40 yds →. Concerned about getting to my accommodations before dark, I hesitated, barely choosing to follow the arrow back to the steep steps up through a space in the hedgerow. Slipping on the moist stones, I climbed to a gravel driveway, re-emerging into brilliant afternoon sunlight.

Blinded momentarily, I looked around, not sure of where I was or where to go.

A lovely elderly man with sparkling eyes appeared out of nowhere.

"Hello, can I help you?"

"Hello…I'm looking for the Well."

"Of course you are!" he smiled. "Step over that stile. Follow the path across the field and down to the bottom of the hill. Take as long as you like. Would you like to join us for a glass of sherry when you come back up?"

"I would love that! Thank you."

Feeling welcomed, I made my way to the bottom of the hill. I saw a rusty wrought iron gate on my right.

I paused and slowly opened the gate.

Alsia Well.

This sacred stone well was tucked into an overgrown hillside, lush with green hedges and grasses. Her gently overflowing waters were trickling down into the creek below. A clootie tree on the left was decorated in multicolored ribbons, dangles, and bracelets, holding visitor's prayers and intentions. Awed into a grateful reverence, I quietly knelt down. I dipped my hands into her cool waters and gently splashed my face. I relaxed some more and sat at her feet. I breathed in her beauty. I was in the presence of the sacred feminine, the goddess herself.

A transcendent peace, calm, and beauty filled me.

From the fear and doubt that consumed me only a few hours earlier, I sat now on the threshold of another world, sourced from the core of Earth herself. I allowed myself to sink deeply on to the moist ground, held in her Love. A place of time and no time. I became like the Well – sourced, open, flowing, and alive.

Alsia Well is the original goddess well in western Cornwall, the only well not discovered and renamed by the Church after a saint. Lovingly cared for by Trevor, the gentle man at the top of the hill, this Well has been a sacred site for pagans and lay people alike for hundreds of years. Some came for fertility and healing, others for ceremony and celebration, all to experience the magic of the Well first hand.

With gratitude, I walked back up the hill, and enjoyed what would become the first of many glasses of sherry and cups of tea with Trevor. Little did I know that my path, my pilgrimage, and my life would change this day and that Alsia Well would become the center of my journey.

Determined at this point to continue on my planned journey, I walked eastward for the next several days, naively confident that I would reach the holy grail of Glastonbury several hundred miles in the distance. Just when I was sure I had it all figured out, and was on the verge of trudging up a steep hill, I heard someone calling my name.

"Sarah! Sarah!"

From the last house in the small village, a woman excitedly waved her arms.

"Sarah!! It's you!"

Sheila, a woman I had met two days earlier at a cafe during a torrential rain storm, ran down to greet me.

"Sarah, come along. You are staying with us. We have a guest room for you with a lovely hot bath. I insist."

I had a choice: to be stubborn and soldier on, or to surrender and accept the invitation. I opted for the guest room and hot bath.

Unaware at the time, I was literally called off the acceptable, tried and true pilgrimage path. For several more years, I tried to stay on the linear path and head east, to walk toward the predetermined destination. Each time, however, I would be called back to walk the same initial miles of the Mary Michael Way. It felt like I was magnetically pulled back to this small, specific area of land with its public footpaths and sacred sites, as though I was meant to walk here, and only here. I could only go so far east before the paths curved back around on themselves, bringing me back to Alsia Well.

Ah! The magic and the mystery of the spiral path. The power of the true healing path.

Alsia Well became the center of my experience. Every year for the next seven years, I would return to Alsia, often by myself or with a friend, sometimes leading a small group of pilgrims, and one time with my youngest daughter, to sit quietly on the damp stones at the Well's opening. I would immerse my hands and feet into her clear waters that had only just risen up from the depths of the earth and gently engage with her, asking for and listening to guidance.

One year, I actually received a dreamcatcher charm that was almost buried in the wet soil near my feet. I carried it with me during my time there, catching my dreams, and returning it with gratitude on the last day.

At the end of each visit to the Well, I would slowly, reluctantly trudge back up the hill, with a promise to return again. I would then find Trevor for another cup of tea and engaging conversation. We became friends over the years, and I even attended his memorial service when he passed in 2019.

From the Well, I would walk a loose spiral of paths that radiated out into the surrounding landscape to eventually connect and incorporate eight other sacred sites in her sphere. The sacred well expanded to include a *fogou* (underground stone chambers), two *càrns* (pile of stones set up as a marker, monument, or memorial of some kind), a cave, a creek, an ancient grandmother tree, two stone circles and another holy well. Each year I would walk the same circular twenty-five miles. I no longer had to figure out which way to go, so I began to experience "walking deeply," a practice that developed and emerged out of my walking these same paths over and over again. I became more intimate with the energies, wisdom, and beauty of the land, the sites, and the paths, so much so that I developed a strong desire to move and live there. The sites quietly beckoned me to engage with them through presence, prayer, writing, and song.

Over time, the paths developed into a coherent spiral that both held and opened me to become more available to the inherent natural and cosmic energies, above and below. Most unexpectedly and surprisingly, this deep and repetitive walking actually activated and opened a portal to an ancient body of feminine wisdom and knowledge, revealing a hidden pilgrimage tradition buried deep in the spiral.

To walk a spiral path is actually a feminine pilgrimage. We do not need to walk far or fast. Rather, we are called on and reminded to walk slowly, deliberately and deeply, wherever we are. While this spiral path and these sacred sites have actually provided me with the map and the pathway I needed to connect with my true self, the spiral path is actually available for all of us, both within and outside of ourselves. It is both an inner and an outer journey, accessible simply through the asking.

As a busy and involved wife and daughter and mother of four children, I had lost my way in the midst of my responsibilities, roles, and busy-ness. I had forgotten that as a woman, all I had to do was go within to touch the divine. I needed an opportunity to step out of my normal everyday life. I wanted an external experience to activate and remind me of what always and already existed within me, and to heal this separation I felt deep within my being. Walking sacred pilgrimage became that opportunity.

The journey transformed from a pilgrimage with an external

distant destination into a spiral path with its focus in the center of the spiral, not as a destination, but as the center of my experience out of which all else revolved and evolved. Alsia Well, at the center of this spiral, provided me with an unexpected focus to organize myself around—to walk about, return to, be resourced by—and experience a divine reflection of myself. Perhaps this is what a sacred site provides us with—an opportunity to see and experience ourselves anew, differently, reverently, sacredly. The Well became the mirror for the restoration of the core of my being, a healing that continues to transform me to this day.

What started out as a journey to reconnect with my roots became an unexpected and profound multiyear pilgrimage to reconnect with my core. It's not the center I had imagined when I first stepped on to the path seven years earlier at Carn Lês Boel. This goes way beyond family, ancestors, and nationality yet somehow includes them all. I now experience a belonging and a wholeness that did not exist before, but is integrated into who I am. My diastasis is healed. My core muscles are becoming stronger. More often than not, I move and choose from within rather than looking outside of myself. My relationship with my mother is softening and opening. Even my relationship with the masculine is healing, a shift I did not expect or see coming.

With my inner core reestablished, I have become like Alsia Well—sourced, rooted, open, flowing, and alive. My life force wells up from deep within me, deep from within the Earth. I remember, and I embody. I can be anywhere and be home. Centered in the core of my being, I walk the spiral path. I deepen into myself as I open and step into the unknown, inviting and allowing myself to flow with the magic and mystery of life.

WORKSHEET: ANOTHER STEP ON YOUR SPIRAL PATH

OFFERED BY SARAH HOSKIN

T he spiral path actually exists wherever we are, both within and outside of ourselves. This gives us an opportunity and invitation to create and walk a sacred path wherever we are. We do not have to travel thousands of miles or leave our own country. A spiral path can easily and simply emerge out of normality, everydayness, right alongside the familiar.

- I invite you to go outside and step into Nature, out in the wild, a city park, or even in your own backyard.
- Allow yourself to gravitate toward a "site"– a tree, a flower garden, a stone, a park bench—as a starting point. Be with your chosen spot, or the spot that chose you! Breathe. Be curious. What do you notice? What do you feel?
- Slowly radiate out, touching and connecting with different "sites," touchstones along the way, a fallen tree, or perhaps a rock, a clump of grass, or anything that catches your eye or you feel drawn toward. Start with one or two sites.

- Add a site each visit, every day for a week or over a month.
- At each site, breathe. Be curious. What do you notice? What do you feel? What are you aware of?

It does not matter what or where you are drawn to. What is important is to open and experience each site, and allow yourself to be drawn to the next stop along the path.

Keep it simple. There is no right or wrong way to do this.

After you feel done, notice what your experience was.

Notice what you are feeling now, having walked in a spiral.

_____

_____

_____

Return to this same area and walk the path again. Perhaps a few times, or every day for a week. Or every season.

What is the same? What changes?

_____

_____

_____

Notice what happens when you return.

Does it feel different? Or has it just returned to being normal, no longer extraordinary? If it still feels special, be curious. Why?

_____

_____

Notice. Be curious. Feel. Receive. Give thanks.

What, if anything, has changed in you?

_____

_____

_____

SARAH HOSKIN

Born in England and raised in the United States, Sarah Hoskin is an intuitive guide and coach, a blogger and author, and a lover of both sacred and daily walks.

A lifetime walker, she has walked pilgrimage paths in Spain and France as well as the U.K., developing a special affinity for the public footpaths and sacred sites in southwestern Cornwall.

Sarah has led groups on pilgrimages in Glastonbury and Cornwall in the U.K., and chakra and labyrinth walks in the U.S. Walking and writing about the spiral path continues to guide and lead her to new adventures in life and love.

Sarah invites and guides women to the Spiral Path, the inner and outer journeys that connect us with the core of our feminine essence and, in turn, provide the foundation from which to live an extraordinary, fulfilling, and creative life.

linktr.ee/sarahhoskin

JOURNEY TO WHOLENESS

SHAWNA BURKHOLDER

For the first time in my life, I was on an adventure that wasn't planned out to the very hour.

I'd been on the road for two months, and that morning I woke up in the nearly vacant hostel. The vinyl covered mattress squeaked as I got out of bed to peek out the window. No snow yet, but it was on the way over the Sierra Mountains in southern California.

I had only packed what would fit in my car: a mix-match of clothes from one fancy dress to hiking boots, the bare minimum of camping equipment, which I hadn't needed so far, and my journals.

Due to space constraints, what I did not have was winter clothing, which made me ever so thankful to have found a little second-hand clothing store, where I was able to score a puffy ski jacket.

Like most of the towns I had visited so far, I would venture out to explore on foot, and ideally find a coffee shop to talk with locals and journal. Journaling was my way of processing all that had led me to this point, and an outlet for exploring my values and dreams.

Looking back, my first week on the road felt like a vacation. No work responsibilities or deadlines. My first stop was at my brother's home outside of Seattle, Washington. I could tell he was holding back judgment and concern for my loose plan to travel south along the West Coast, then across the southern states. I hoped that I would reach Key West in Florida by October to celebrate my birthday, then travel north along the East Coast to make my way to New York City by New Year's Eve so I could watch the ball drop in Times Square. This flight of fancy, I imagined, would take me about nine months.

As I ventured on, from Washington to Idaho and then Montana, the cold reality hit me. I was alone, and this was no vacation. Several times I wondered if I should turn back and play it safe by getting a job and an apartment or keep going forward into the unknown.

I thought back on what brought me to that point, seeking the courage to keep moving forward.

It's early summer, and the sound of the ceiling fan is the only thing breaking the silence as I lay on the floor of my empty house, salty tears running down my face. It echoes the thumping of my heart in my chest. I feel so lost and wonder how my life became a train wreck. This house is no longer mine. The new owners are moving in this weekend. My eighteen-year relationship ended on peaceful terms and because of this I wonder if I've made the wrong decision. Perhaps we could have repaired our broken relationship. But, like the house, it's too late to go back. On top of that, I quit my job.

Exactly what brought me to the point of walking away from my job, relationship, and home in order to travel? What may have appeared to be a snap decision to up-turn my entire life was the result of years of built-up discontent. Years of doing what was expected and worried that I wasn't good enough in my relationship pulled me off course from being my authentic self. I had a growing feeling that something was missing in my life. I couldn't put my finger on it at that time, but knew until I discovered what was missing, I would not be whole.

I had been on the fast track to burnout at work for years. I held a prominent position at the second largest charity in my community. I was well known, attending networking events, advocating for policies and laws that supported equality and inclusion, and we held some of the most successful and well-loved fundraisers every year. I convinced myself that my worth was equal to what I produced. And the more I produced, the more value I had. This made reaching, even exceeding, revenue goals the prize which validated 60-hour work weeks. This status and visibility created the illusion of a charmed life.

But I had become a workaholic, mistaking job success for self-worth and meaningful contribution. It was normal for me to be the first person in the office and not leave until dark, often missing dinner at home. Still not able to get everything done, I started working full days on Saturday. I was fully aware that I needed to delegate more, but to whom? All the extra time at work took its toll on an already strained relationship at home.

Then it happened.

The morning of our largest fundraiser, my 98-year-old grandmother passed away. I was grateful to be at her side, holding her hand and telling her it was going to be okay and that she would be with grandpa soon. Her passing wasn't unexpected, as she'd been receiving hospice care for several months; within an hour, I had all the paperwork signed and arrangements made to 'take care of her body.'

I felt gutted. Pushing down my shame for not being fully present and honoring her transition, I turned my attention to work.

My job stress combined with grief led me to become utterly, completely burned out. Due to the post-event responsibilities, I was unable to take bereavement leave. Work became a trail of missed deadlines and unmet production targets. I wasn't sleeping, my health was deteriorating, and my personal relationships were suffering even more.

So I quit.

My first instinct was to get another job right away. However, I needed time to grieve and reset my priorities. I wasn't sure I even wanted to stay in the same field of work, so taking some time off seemed like the smart thing to do. This added even more pressure on my relationship and the level of dysfunction became undeniable.

We both knew for years that we were operating at what I call the 'lowest common denominator.' Our process for making decisions resulted in a diluted compromise. Something as simple as choosing a restaurant for dinner devolved into excuses that it was too expensive, too far away, too (fill in the blank), and we'd end up staying home eating leftovers or ordering pizza. There was no growth in our relationship as it was based on being, and staying, comfortable doing nothing. It was time for us to call it quits, too.

Without being tied to a job or relationship, I realized I could live anywhere I wanted. I was free to move. But where? I had no idea. So, rather than buying another house or renting an apartment, I put my belongings in storage. The idea to travel came when I read this statistic in a long-forgotten blog post, "The average adventure traveler is no longer a 28-year-old male, but a 47-year-old female. And she wears a size 12 dress." I found a reason that got me up and moved me forward.

Yes, I was jobless, spouseless, and homeless; yet instead of afraid I felt free.

There were no more outside influences to distract me. Each mile I pushed forward left the stressed out, unfulfilled person I was in my wake. With each town and experience, I grew braver and felt a renewed sense of purpose. When I looked up into the rear-view mirror it was with the resolve that I would not repeat past mistakes. The road ahead held the hope and promise of a fulfilling life.

It wasn't easy at first. I was sad, lonely, and very uncertain. Two weeks in, I was in Idaho when the doubt and insecurities became the loudest. I spent three full days never leaving the hotel room, subsisting on power bars and vending machine water, paralyzed with my new reality. The self-soothing stories I was feeding myself of being on vacation or going on sabbatical unwound to reveal themselves as lies.

Finally, the tears came, but the answers did not.

For days I was racked with grief moving from denial into despair.

What had I done?

Do I go back?

I missed my grandma, my former colleagues, my friends and even my ex. I had never felt so alone. Letting go had never been so hard.

It was in Montana that I hit my lowest point.

Still isolating myself, I stopped at the store to buy food and alcohol, then sequestered myself in the hotel room. With only TV to keep me company, I decided to take a bath. I sat in the tub, drinking wine and crying. For the first time ever, thoughts of self-harm crept in. That scared me. It was my wake-up call. Yes, my life was a mess, but I chose to take this journey of self-discovery. I gave myself a good scolding. I had lots to live for, even if I couldn't clearly see what was ahead of me.

That was my turning point.

To drive that point home, the next day I visited Yellowstone National Park, specifically to see the Old Faithful Geyser. As the crowd grew, I was struck by the fact that I could hear three different languages being spoken within proximity of where I was sitting. In that moment, I felt my heart opening as I was filled with the sense of the greater humanity of our world. Here I was, at the time a very lonely individual, surrounded by hundreds of people who had traveled thousands of miles to have a shared experience that was rare in our natural world.

Then, in Reno, Nevada, my AirBnB hosts recommended a few places for me to experience. By chance, there was a community festival. A group of five ladies noticed that I was solo, and struck up a conversation. They were locals and more than delighted to show this tourist around town. Together we explored galleries and boutiques, and enjoyed dinner in a quirky restaurant. I felt warmly welcomed into a spontaneous circle of sisterhood. Once again, my heart was connecting.

One town after another, I was connecting again. In a tiny town where the post office was also the pharmacy and a yarn shop, I spent hours talking with the sweet older lady who was also happy to have my company. At another point, in an amusement park, surrounded by laughing families, I was joyfully skipping along to the next ride!

There were tests along the way, too.

As I was driving through the mountain range, I was gripped by fear of driving off the road down the cliff. Heart pounding, hands sweating, I gripped the steering wheel as if my life depended on it. Fear was getting the best of me. I reasoned to myself that if thousands of people travel this road without dying, I can too. Finally, I couldn't stand it any longer; the drop-off on my right side was getting steeper by the mile. Up ahead on my left, I saw a pull-out carved into the side of the mountain that might fit two cars. Praying that there would be no oncoming traffic from the bend ahead, I made the snap decision to cross the center line and parked. Soaked in sweat and shaking, I practiced deep breathing, as I pondered my choices, "I can't stay here indefinitely. I have to decide. Do I keep going or turn back? Hmmm, where have I heard that before?"

Ten minutes later, I calmed my nerves and decided to continue. Cautiously I navigated getting back onto the roadway in between passing cars. Imagine my relief and elation when only a few miles past that bend the terrain mostly flattened out and there were no more severe drop-offs along the road. I was ecstatic. A feeling of resilience and empowerment washed over me. If I could do this, anything was possible.

All told, I was on the road for four months when I had that 'knowing' feeling that it was time to go home. My grand plan for driving the perimeter of the United States no longer felt necessary, but a nice idea to reconsider someday.

After driving through seven states and staying in numerous towns, that emptiness I felt had vanished.

Sitting in the coffee shop, I see that the predicted snow has finally arrived. I text my brother, "I'm ready to come home. Can I stay with you while I get settled?"

I have plenty of time on the long drive back to think about where to live and getting a job. I'm not worried, as I trust it will all come together. For the first time in a very long time, I'm smiling on the outside and the inside. I am happy. I know who I am. I feel whole.

WORKSHEET: ANOTHER STEP ON YOUR SPIRAL PATH

OFFERED BY SHAWNA BURKHOLDER

Here are three prompts for self-discovery. Use all three or the one that most resonates with you.

<u>Timeline Map</u>: Ideal for creative/visual people.

On a separate piece of paper of any size, using lots of colors and pictures, note significant milestones in your life up until now. Then, add milestones you would like to reach in your future (much like a vision board). This does not have to be linear—just to get you started, write on the lines below those milestones that immediately come to mind.

_____

_____

_____

<u>Hot Pen Journaling</u>: Ideal for people who prefer to write their thoughts.

Your prompt is: *It is (a date three years in the future) and I am so happy and grateful now that...*

For five minutes each, write without stopping about the future of these four areas of your life: relationships, wealth and abundance, well-being, and career/vocation. In the future, anything and everything IS possible. Don't get bogged down in the 'how.' Write fast and furious about what would make you most happy in these areas.

Time Machine: Ideal for those people who prefer to move.

Stand up.

Step into your imaginary time machine.

Rotate counterclockwise, three turns for each year forward into the future. In the future you meet a good friend you haven't seen in years, and she asks, "What have you been up to?" Bursting with excitement, you respond, *"I am so happy and grateful now that..."* and share all the wonderful things you have done or experienced in the past three years.

What are you grateful for in the past three years?

SHAWNA BURKHOLDER

Shawna Burkholder is a Life Strategist who helps over-achieving professionals experiencing burnout to reset priorities, regain time, and revitalize their relationships.

At the heart of Shawna's approach is her belief that everyone deserves to lead a fulfilling life. Her programs offer a supportive and empowering path out of struggle mode and into time and money freedom.

Shawna's credentials include being an Elite Mentorship Forum Licensed Trainer, a Whole Person Certified Coach, and Crisis Communication Certification/Instructor with the American Red Cross. She holds a Strategic Communication Certification from Washington State University, where she also earned her Bachelor of Psychology.

Additionally, Shawna lives in the Pacific Northwest and is a seasoned marathoner with over twelve finishes and six half marathon finishes.

linktr.ee/shawna_burkholder

THE SACRED PAUSE

JOANNA LYNN STEFFEL

The sounds of sirens…. The swishing of fabric…The sense of urgency… An inaudible cry of a broken heart…

These are the flashes of what I can remember as my body fell into a shock of sensory overwhelm. What just happened? One moment, I am gleefully skipping down this marble staircase to my new beginning and new life at a long-awaited arrival to Siena Heights University. Another moment, I am sprawled out at the bottom of the steps in pain.

This is my first (and last) time using this beautiful staircase, which flared out at the bottom. There must have been some moisture on the steps, and in my hurried pace, my foam flip flop met the slick marble, which combined with the speed of my pace, was a recipe for disaster. This was not how I had anticipated my first day of classes going.

The scientific and mathematical side of my brain often runs the calculations of how I missed two steps and fell squarely on my right ankle. I have watched enough true crime documentaries to know how lethal even a two-step drop can be. A counterbalance or shift in my weight a few degrees or inches in one direction or another and I could have cracked my head open.

My faith offers another, more reassuring version of the story, one that tells me that my guardian angel is with me and has helped me land in a safer way. I felt a presence with me on those stairs and I couldn't shake a sense of protection.

After the initial shock wore off, I assessed the scene.

Great, I am all alone. I know I have been clumsy before and been shitty to my ankles, too. Twisting them and spraining them too many times to count. The pain hasn't registered yet; the adrenaline is still pumping through my veins. So I do the careful dance of shifting my weight. A shockwave of pain and realization vibrates through my body, "Holy shit, Joanna! You did more than just sprain it this time."

All I could do now was wait for a Good Samaritan to come to my aid.

As I waited for what seemed like an eternity, I felt like a damn fool with a self-fulfilling prophecy. Just a day before, Trudy McSorely, Dean of Students, and Nurse Norma noted that Siena had a great working relationship with the community resources like ambulance and staff at Bixby Hospital, stating that it never fails, someone always ends up needing these services within the first week of classes. I had half-heartedly joked to myself that, knowing my luck, I'd be that student who got the golden ticket for an ambulance ride!!

I am shaken back to being at the bottom of the stairs when a member of the custodial staff asks if I am alright. I calmly and sweetly say that I'm not, that I think I've broken my ankle. She rushes back up the stairs to make a phone call. I shake my head and hope we don't end up on twin gurneys.... SLOW DOWN!!!!

It was clear as day. I needed to slow down, but so did the world around me.

Next thing I know, I see the familiar faces of Trudy and Nurse Norma. Trudy says she can't reach my mom. She asks who else she could call. I give her my sister's number. My mom probably wasn't home quite yet from teaching, but my sister would know how to hunt her down. How the hell did we survive without a cell phone??

Nurse Norma tells me an ambulance is on the way. She props

and stabilizes my ankle trying to make me as comfortable as possible.

The next few days take on a life of their own as the frenzy of fixing me begins. It seems like much of a blur. It's only now in the passenger's seat of my parents' van driving down from Adrian, Michigan, back to Bryan, Ohio, that I can string together what happened this week.

I am fading in and out of sleep trying to fight off the remnants of the anesthesia. I hate that feeling of grogginess and being out of control. Monday the fall and ER. Tuesday discussion with the orthopedic surgeon. I broke that ankle and not in just a way that I'd wear a cast... oh no, I did her a good one... I'd be a bionic person... a plate and four screws and a pin to stabilize it as it healed for 13 weeks. Then, a second surgery to remove the pin and replace the cast with a walking boot.

Wednesday... we are now on Wednesday, post-surgery.

I had not let this detour in my life even really set in yet. I was in crisis-management mode. Making decisions right and left out of sheer necessity. Ugh! The pain drugs are starting to wear off and so is my patience. I ask if we can pull over in Lyons, Ohio, at the convenience store for a snack and drink.

Now, this was not just any convenience store or pit stop. Lyons is my mother's hometown, a midway point. The convenience store was the original site of my grandfather's car dealership and across the street my grandparents' house. Here was a safe place, a sacred holding space. I sent my parents on a fool's errand to hunt for provisions to provide me comfort, but a deeper solace came from being in this place where my family once gathered. While staring at the droplet of water falling down the window, I was alone and ready to release the tears that I had bravely held back until this moment. They began to pour just like skies above already had. I have always found it easier to cry when the heavens do too. The dam had been broken.

I screamed and bawled. I cursed God. I thought that this was my turn to have something work out.

"Why? Why the fuck did you call me to Siena with this deep

knowing that it was home, just to rip it away from me? What the
hell did this all mean? I was sickened by the call and finally
answering it, just to have it thrown right back in my face. What did I
do to invoke this next level chaotic mess in my life? When was I
finally able to walk the primrose path? Goddamn Goddamn
Goddamn."

I gather my composure as my parents walk back to the van. I
dive into the bag of chips and gulp down ginger ale. I pop a vicodin
and beg for the Sandman to take me away from it all.

As I heal, the rhythm of my recovery changes, too. There's more
time to think…to feel…to imagine. In this forced pause, I start
seeing the divine order and timing of all things.

I pull out my journal and write.

Week 5 of Recovery, Tuesday, September 19th

*Dear God, I read Psalm 139 today. My reflection on this is that even when
I left from active participation in the Catholic Church, I couldn't hide from you
or your calling. You called me to Siena. I even know this now five weeks into this
dreadful experience, you have been with me like always. I can't hide from you as
much as I try.*

*I am sorry for cursing you out so many times about this condition. I know
you can sympathize with the fact that something was ignited that night that I
went to Mass with my roommate Denise. The eve of the fall. I had embraced St.
Dominic's trailblazing spirit from the story in the homily. I felt the reigniting of
the Holy Spirit's flame in my heart. That is why I was so crushed when the fall
happened. I wanted to get back to my ministry calling. I know I tried to hide
from it by going to Adrian College and majoring in Mathematics. The time there
was needed, and woke me up to some issues that needed to be addressed. That's
what led me to Diane and to falling in love with therapy. Hence the switch in
major. I have been looking at the course catalog. I know I have to take a religion
class. I just want to get it out of the way. You know my resistance to all things
Catholic. I am still working through my issues with the things I have seen in the
Church… i.e. the wounding Father did not only to me in denying me
confirmation due to my tonsillitis or the way he turned away so many from the*

Church when he used some not so savory ways to ask for money for the $4 million Church. That was a last straw for me, that and the priest allegations of sexual abuse with the Church globally. I could not participate in it any longer. I know you understand. Church politics takes away from the beauty you provide us.

There was something different though about Father Tom, the priest at Siena. He reminded me of the priest we had when I was growing up and going to Catholic school. Maybe on my return to Siena, I'll try going to Mass again. It couldn't hurt and I am grateful for him and Ian coming to do my room blessing and the administering anointing of the sick sacrament and communion. Even though that room isn't where I reside now. I do have the cross hanging on the wall here at mom and dad's. It gave me solace before the surgery and even now. But for now, I think I'll commit to taking Relational Ethics… that sounds the least Catholic. Reading novels that talk about how people relate with one another and with you…that sounds like my jam. Give me credit and allow me to find my way in how I express my faith in you and help guide me in finding community.

Until tomorrow your loving daughter, Joanna.

P.S. Can you do something about the itch of the cast because I really don't know how I will last another eight weeks of this!!

P.P.S. Thanks to Mom for making my 21st birthday as special as it could be, all things considered. It wasn't the 21st I had envisioned like going out and drinking with my college friends. I guess 22 will have to be a big party!

Dominican Hall Room 202

Relational Ethics with Joseph Raab

I'm thirty minutes early. I peek into the classroom. There is a slender khakis-and-polo-wearing professor; Gene Wilder energy without the crazy hair. He places a syllabus at each seat in the U shape configuration. I knock. I announce myself, saying I know I am early but wondered if it was ok if I came in and scope out a prime seat. I point to my walking boot and look for an extra chair to prop up my foot. I select the seat closest to the door because I can see everything in the room that way, including the treetops from the window outside.

Professor Raab asks what had happened and I share how I had

fallen down the stairs in Sacred Heart Hall right below Touchdown Jesus. I joke that I should have high-fived Jesus for good luck like the jocks do before any game. He chuckles, acknowledging the good sense of humor I have about my setback. Laughter, after all, is the best kind of medicine.

I pick up the syllabus and read the journey of where the Relational Ethics course will take us. Thomas Keating's book *The Human Condition* tops the list. I have my copy already and I flip through the opening. I'm intrigued by the phrase Divine Therapy and pondered the appropriateness and synchronicity of reading that phrase in this exact moment.

Little did I know then that this course, this professor and this thin book was going to change the direction of my life.

I take a sacred breath in and release it with a sigh.

I am back home, ready to embrace what God has planned for me. No longer anxious or angry, just in sheer acceptance of everything that happens for a reason.

I am ready to see what unfolds in the Divine timing and order of things.

WORKSHEET: ANOTHER STEP ON YOUR SPIRAL PATH

OFFERED BY JOANNA LYNN STEFFEL

A book that helped me bridge the gap in seemingly opposing viewpoints of psychology and theology is *The Human Condition: Contemplation and Transformation* by Thomas Keating. In this book he asks two big questions: Who am I, and where do I belong?

Keating was a Catholic trappist monk who extensively studied psychology. He coined the term Divine Therapy. My story was a hard therapy session with the Divine, but it was also transformational, meditative, and reflective.

Paraphrasing one of my favorite quotes from the book, we can view the process of spiritual growth like a spiral staircase that moves us towards the increasingly profound humiliation of the false self, which leads us to inner freedom and inner resurrection.

Make a mystic choice here.

Journal, doodle, paint, collage, or create another way to express, acknowledge, and witness your life as a spiral staircase.

Where are you on the spiral staircase? Are you at the bottom facing a humiliation of a false self? Are you climbing with grace and ease towards your true self? (Know that wherever you are is in Divine Perfection).

_____

_____

_____

How can you view your spiritual journey as a movement towards inner freedom and inner resurrection? What does that mean to you?

_____

_____

_____

Extra Credit: Incorporate themes from Psalm 139:1-18. (Divine knowing you wholly and completely, hiding out from the Divine, Divine plan for your life).

How does this shift your perspective?

_____

_____

_____

Where are you finding the Divine in your life?

_____

_____

_____

How have you tried to escape Spirit's calling to your Divine purpose?

_____

_____

_____

In what ways can you surrender and trust in the Divine timing and order of your unfolding path and pace?

_____

_____

_____

JOANNA LYNN STEFFEL

Joanna Lynn Steffel identifies as a Queer Catholic Mystic.

One of her favorite meditative practices is drinking tea. Joanna sees herself as a unique blend. She is steeped in spiritual traditions and rituals from her upbringing, equal parts Austrian Catholic and U.K. Protestant, with an ounce of Agent of Chaos, a splash of Veritas, and, for good measure, a sprinkle of Creatrix.

Joanna has found herself seeking universal truth through world religions. With an obsession of story as a tool for healing, she loves to interweave the stories of the cosmos and self through her study of astrology.

In her extensive training in both Pastoral Counseling and metaphysics, she has cultivated an integrative shamanic narrative approach to help others heal the wounds of the past and gain confidence in the present so they are able to make their future dreams come true.

linktr.ee/beautifullychaoticmystics

PULLING THE PLUG ON PEOPLE-PLEASING

JOSETTE MILLS

D o I have any PEOPLE-PLEASERS in the building? Don't be afraid, go ahead, raise your hand *with* me! I am a recovering people-pleaser and celebrate my daily wins in making marginal strides against those behaviors intentionally.

I'm here to share a story about a time when I learned the hard way that Toni Morrison's quote "If you want to fly, you have to give up the shit that weighs you down" was my REALITY.

There was a time when I worked three full-time jobs just to be able to please my friends and family. One seemingly normal day at my DAY job, the room suddenly started spinning. It felt like a personal tornado was in full effect, and then I vomited. The last thing I remembered before I blacked out was my coworker shouting my name...the next thing I knew, I was in the emergency room of a nearby hospital. I looked up at my family and burst into tears because at that present moment, I didn't know my fate.

Loads of tests and multiple conversations later, I was discharged with instructions that hit me in the gut like a powerful Bruce Lee kick. I was devastated when the doctor said, "You have to stay out of work for two to three weeks."

This felt like a life sentence because, sadly, my first thought was,

"How can I continue to take care of everybody being out of work for two to three weeks?" My thoughts never went to my health, and this was a wake-up call God sent me.

There was one more moment to dread: the prescription for medication. My fate rested in the support of a drug I did not want to take. I was torn.

At home, I sat with my thoughts for the remainder of that evening. I had to face the HARD reality: If I wanted to LIVE, I had to give up the shit that was weighing me down. This self-imposed stress that I created as comfort and a means to feel worthy, to matter, to feel validated, was draining the possibility of longevity for my life.

Being home for two to three weeks was the perfect time to ignite a plan to please myself. I had to both pull back the curtains to stare into the darkness of uncertainty and I had to push forward in a new direction.

My first step was to DECIDE what I wanted because things could not stay the way they were. I knew that meant taking off the SUPERWOMAN cape I wore like a badge of honor because it was not only very exhausting, it was also killing me, literally.

One question kept weighing me down, "What am I actually afraid of?"

Some thoughts scared the hell out of me.

What if they don't love me anymore?

What if they don't want to be bothered with me anymore?

What if....

All the *what if's* drove me to misery. I even told myself that our relationships would end if I'm not "doing" anything for them. Revisiting these thoughts now, it truly feels and sounds disturbing...all these made-up stories created in the falsehood of my busy "making everything about me" mind.

Here's the thing: It was *not* the truth. I had no evidence to support any of it and, in reality, it was an entire production that was built on a non-existent turn of events.

What I knew to be true was that if I kept doing the same thing, getting the same results, that was psychotic. I had to stop fighting for my excuses. As the saying goes, "How you do anything, is how you do everything. Everywhere you go, there you are."

I saw the same patterns at work. I would take on additional tasks from my coworkers so they would accept me and find real value in my friendship. I would be the first one in, last one out to show my dedication and commitment to the company, going above and beyond to prove my worth.

I had to switch things up. I had to release the tendency for perfection. I had to embrace the idea that my greatest gifts may come wrapped in sandpaper, something one of my mentors, Lisa Nichols, once pointed out.

Google became a best friend as I discovered that my symptoms and behaviors matched a condition known as *people pleasing*. The quest to know more resulted in frequent visits to my favorite happy places— the library and Barnes & Noble Bookstore. The psychology and self-help sections invited my mind and heart to go deeper, get curious, ask tough questions and be uncomfortable in order to heighten my awareness.

All sorts of modalities enticed me: Emotional intelligence; boundaries; self-regulation; self-love; meditation; breathwork; movement; emotional release, and coaching, to name just a few. I'm an extremist...you name it, I try to learn everything there is to know about the subject at hand.

During my rediscover, reconnect, and reignite journey, I read several books, and three impacted my life the most: *The Body Keeps Score* by Dr. Bessel Van Der Kolk; *Emotional Intelligence* by David Goleman, and *Emotional Alchemy*, by Tara Bennett-Goleman. They broadened my perspective about what I was doing to *myself* and those I loved, and offered ways to intentionally alter my life forever by raising the bar on my emotional intelligence.

I began to go within my mind, body, and soul to explore the root of my people-pleasing behaviors because "How did I get here?" kept playing over and over in my mind.

Being new to the empty-nester life left too much time to be with myself. That scared me because when I was being a caregiver/mother figure to my siblings and cousins, a teen parent, an adoptive parent, a wife and a caregiver to grandparents, I had little time to know what my own desires looked or felt like. Pouring into others from an empty cup for so many years left such a depleted container that I no longer knew what lit me up. It was such a numb place to be in.

In a weird kind of way, it made sense to me to continue to be everything to them, *according to my definition of what they needed,* so that I stayed prevalent in their lives, so I could stay relevant in my own life. They were all grown up, and I was still vicariously living through them. The reality was that they had their own lives to live, and so did I.

The first epiphany of many came when I was journaling one day, capturing my childhood experiences that more than likely were inhibitors of what was showing up now in my adult life.

While thinking through ages one to ten, I thought of life experiences where I felt abandoned because visits from my dad were not consistent…I felt ashamed when kids teased me about my mom's drug use…I felt neglected when I didn't receive what other kids had…I felt judged because I was a teenage mom of two kids and the societal expectations would discount me to be a statistic, a product of my environment, someone on welfare, abusing drugs and alcohol.

Considering the aforementioned and other chain of events, my thoughts were "Of course" I would think, feel, and behave the way I was behaving.

More importantly, I reflected, I had to accept myself for who I was: the good, the bad and the ugly. I had to accept that I was a flawed individual. That was normal. I did nothing wrong. I was a human having a human experience. I began to intentionally explore opportunities that could help me work through the neck-down numb feeling I had lived in for so long, and instead move to a place of contentment and fulfillment.

It was not a one and done process. Making space for ME in my life required that I put healthy boundaries in place. Two letters, N and O with a period [.], became a complete sentence. *No.*

It was not easy. Looking in a mirror, I practiced saying no in different ways. I adjusted my tone and cringed while projecting and feeling the assumed disappointment. I practiced ways to say no... ways to say it that felt good in my body without creating a smoke screen of an explanation because it soothed them or myself, or eased the weight of my "no" with a reason attached. Fulfilling their instant gratification became a thing of the past. I began to build my belief muscles and learned how to hold myself in high regard. Looking back now, it was SO worth it.

Then there was the trial and error of experimenting with numerous healing modalities. They were my biggest strength builders. I stole back a few moments a day, learning to sit still long enough to meditate, and seconds developed into minutes, slowly but surely. There were times that I felt like nothing was changing, and I wanted to throw in the towel. But I knew that going back to the familiar was no longer optional. I noticed that I was becoming more tolerant to sitting still longer, and my focus sharpened every day. Interruptions lessened, too, because my family saw that I was serious about it. They even said I yelled at them less after sitting like that.

While exploring multiple practitioners of emotional release and movement work, I felt so out of place because other attendees knew the rules, the appropriate attire, the moves and verbal cues, and were free to express themselves as they saw fit. I was judging myself so much, I couldn't fully pay attention, my brain was a huge distraction, but the feeling the practices left in my mind and body called me back quite often. Like a bottle of Pepsi being opened and you hear that *psssst* sound of the air being released. I committed to feeling those emotions and surrendering to the new habits that were forming, so much so that I got certified to teach my favorite modality to other women.

Honestly, it would tickle me to tears when my family would say things like, "You're much calmer!" "You're not going to punish us? What is going on with you?" and "It must be a midlife crisis." That type of unrequested feedback gave me so much fuel to keep going because, though sometimes I may have felt like I was getting nowhere, the proof was in the pudding they were sharing, so I kept going.

Then there was the Emotional Freedom Technique (EFT). It was tough at first because I always felt like I was tapping but expecting some sign that something was happening. But I kept practicing and truly discovered its impact; today, it's still one of my go-tos for both me and my clients.

Reconnecting to myself allowed for a reconnection to my family and community at large. Rediscovering what fell by the wayside was so life giving. And reigniting the desire to dust off my dormant dreams that were withering away filled my heart and soul.

Taking the time to REDISCOVER what I wanted for myself, what could bring *fulfillment* to *me* meant I had to repeatedly *go within* and continually get reacquainted with myself. Experiencing and exploring ways to enhance my self-love muscle and to be more kind to myself, developing better ways to communicate with myself, and adopting principles and habits that offered self-regulation became my new daily, and what is now my lifelong, endeavor. This allowed me to also have better conversations with others, to actually be present in the exchange. Piquing my curiosity for what was possible, exploring, testing, and setting boundaries that also impacted my decision-making and outcomes were extremely important to me. I truly had to release what was in order to create the capacity for what I truly desired.

Tapping into my inner knowing and honoring my worth were key components. I knew I wanted to unapologetically create space and inner peace for the life I was working towards, and I spent time envisioning my desires… my personal cook making my meals, my bedroom view of the ocean, a few steps to a beautiful beach, a wrap-around terrace, having my driver escort me wherever my heart thinks of, and financial freedom to help as many people as I desire in the blink of an eye. Yes, yes!

Surprisingly, though it is a part of the safety message while in flight and yes, this was before COVID 19, putting my mask on first became my rebirth motto. If someone called and requested something of me, I refrained from providing an instant response and redirected them to use their smartphones "smartly" by looking it up. I minimized my commitments to only what "I" truly wanted to do. Embodying that saying "yes" to others was saying "no" to myself reinforced my alignment with my personal boundaries and, eventually, shifted their expectations, too. I still stand by it proudly today.

People always ask how I did this, and I say it's a daily practice that I'm committed to, literally because there's always more to explore. We have to intentionally and unapologetically protect ourselves, without guilt or shame, because life will life us!

Seeing how far I have come is so heartwarming. The most rewarding is seeing how my family is self-sufficient and how my new lifestyle is as comforting as an electric blanket on a cold winter night. It's all about commitment to the end game, refusing to give up on myself, and knowing that I matter, I am enough and I am worthy of all I desire. Even on the days when I may feel like old behaviors creep up, I don't beat myself up. Instead, I give myself grace, course-correct with loving kindness and keep moving forward. My regimen gives me the opportunity to reinvent and reignite myself over and over again.

I hope my story gives you the momentum to adopt these principles and see the outcomes that begin to manifest for you. I invite you to make my mantra your own. Repeat it as you, too, go on your healing journey. Place both hands over your heart and say each one louder: I Matter. I Matter. I MATTER.

WORKSHEET: ANOTHER STEP ON YOUR SPIRAL PATH

OFFERED BY JOSETTE MILLS

Ready to pull the plug on people-pleasing and putting other people's desires ahead of your own? Use these prompts to help you rediscover your passions, reconnect to what matters most to you, and reignite your soul's purpose.

Where do you fall within your list of priorities?

_____

_____

_____

Read this question. *If it's safe, then close your eyes:* What have you left burning on the back burner that needs your attention right now? For example, what's something you've wanted for yourself but haven't done yet or what dream have you deferred?

_____

_____

_____

What would make you feel fulfilled? In your health, career, and relationships?

_____

_____

_____

Are you willing to be committed to yourself to make your thoughts and dreams your reality?

    Yes

    No

    If not, what would help you be in a position to make that a yes?

_____

_____

_____

What provides happiness to your body?

_____

_____

_____

What brings you pleasure?

_____

_____

_____

What excites you? Like, butterflies in your belly...

_____

_____

_____

What brings you joy? Like, hands clapping, legs dancing, huge smiles...

_____

_____

_____

What would you like to <u>rediscover</u> for yourself?

_____

_____

_____

What would you like to <u>reconnect</u> with or do for yourself?

_____

_____

_____

What would you like to <u>reignite</u> with or for yourself?

_____

_____

_____

JOSETTE MILLS

Josette Mills is a Midlife Fulfillment Coach. She is the founder of The School of Midlife Freedom.

Josette's professional coaching and trainings are layered through multiple modalities. She is a Master Certified Life Coach, a Sedona Soul Transformational Coach, Certified Life Coach through The Life Coach School with Brooke Castillo, and is training to be a RTT Certified Therapist with Marisa Peer. Josette is also a licensed Emotional Tour instructor for The Emotional Institute with Bernadette Pleasant and a Level 2 Reiki practitioner.

Josette enjoys seeing the relief in her client's faces when they find what's hidden in their mind and body and fulfill their innermost desires.

Josette is on a mission to serve 1,000 women in the next two years, expanding her impact so that young women can learn from and be guided by graduates of The School of Midlife Freedom.

linktr.ee/josettemills

ALLOWING GRIEF, LISTENING FOR LOVE

ROXANNA FIGUEROA

"We are made of Energy, Sound Vibration, and Light.
It is from whence we come and to where we shall return..."
- Jeralyn Glass with Dylan Sage

I t's a cloudy, cold day. I stand alone, looking out at the calm, majestic deep blue ocean, listening to the waves gently lapping on the shore and feeling the white sand between my toes. A deep sense of calm comes into my heart, and I begin to wonder: *What would it be like to walk in the water and leave this world?*

Today is my mom's birthday. Last week was the last time we spoke. She had called to tell me that she had been admitted to the hospital due to a heart issue and was scheduled for exploratory surgery the next day.

Our conversation felt off. I could sense that she was worried about her upcoming surgery because she asked about my future and the changes I was making. She knew that I had been on a path of healing from the tidbits of information I had previously shared. Typically, our discussions were always centered around her wants and needs, rarely about me and my life. In retrospect, I wish I had shared my journey into healing and the world of crystal alchemy bowls, but instead, I kept the conversation focused on preparing for her scheduled surgery.

"I love you, Mama," I said, hanging up the phone.

"I love you, Muñeca," she replied.

In the middle of the night, her heart struggling to beat, Mom was rushed into emergency surgery. When the surgeon opened her up, he was shocked to see that all four of her coronary arteries were clogged. After a successful quadruple bypass, Mom suffered a heart attack as they were closing her up. A second emergency surgery was performed, this time to insert a series of balloons in her arm, stomach, and leg to help facilitate blood circulation while her heart recovered and rested.

Rushing to the hospital, it felt as if time had stopped. Outside the hospital, the world continued to turn and move on. For me, I knew that nothing would be the same ever again.

I stood at the door, taking everything in. I looked at my mom lying unconscious on the hospital bed, swollen, ghostly pale, with multiple machines hooked up to her. Two nurses ran from machine to machine, moving from one alarm to the next, while the third monitored her respiratory rates. The nurses told me that the next 48 hours were critical. Standing there, fully present, I could feel my heart breaking. Who could have predicted this moment?

Holding her swollen, cold hand, I kissed her forehead and laid my head down next to her, immediately struck by all the moments that had led to this one.

Born in Puerto Rico, Mom moved to New York City, married at the age of twenty and proceeded to have four children, one right after the other, all the while not wanting the responsibility of them. Instead, she was on a quest to fulfill her purpose of being a missionary teacher. After her first divorce, she met my father, had me, and then moved to the West Coast, where she attended Simpson Bible College and Cal State Hayward. Somewhere along the way, after years of physical and mental abuse, she divorced my father. Later, over the years, she married and divorced four more husbands, leaving a trail of heartache, broken relationships, and promises in her wake.

Growing up my mother's daughter wasn't easy. My mom was a clever opportunist with narcissistic tendencies and a loud and boisterous personality. She never had money, so she was always asking or manipulating people into giving her some. We moved every one to two years and never had a stable home. My mom often left us unattended for days at a time with my eldest sister in charge, and eventually, she left for good.

My mother was deeply religious but struggled with rules and authority. While belief in God was her number one value, she would routinely change churches if they did not meet her expectations or values. I used to joke that she changed churches as often as she changed husbands.

Once my mother realized she would not become a missionary teacher, she became a substitute teacher and, ultimately, a caregiver for her parents. She did the best she could with the tools she was given, but we, as her children, suffered through poverty and endured childhood mental and physical abuse, neglect, and abandonment.

On my own path, I had developed my coping mechanism of escape at a young age, not wanting to feel or embody the pain, the loneliness, and the sorrow. I learned to build a shell around my heart like a turtle to protect the little, brown-skinned girl who felt too much. When I discovered booze as a teenager, I drank to escape my pain and stayed on this path for quite some time while simultaneously searching for my purpose. Even through the haze, I knew that I was here to contribute to the healing of the world.

As the years passed, I received my Bachelor's degree in Psychology, worked for several heart-centered, non-profit organizations, and still, I continued to search for my purpose. Finally, in 2019, I had a powerful prediction that foretold of a life-altering decision I would need to make: I could do nothing and end up going down a dark path of booze, or I could choose to go down a path of transformation of the self to the universal self.

Four years have passed since I took a leap of faith and surrendered, leaving the alcohol behind to create a new life. I have embarked upon a personal journey of renewal and healing. I am happily sober and have opened up my channel of intuition, my channel to Source. I left my toxic job and went to school, earning several certifications in coaching, meditation instruction, Reiki, and sound healing. It was when I discovered the healing power of the crystal alchemy bowls that my heart began to heal. When I heard my first performance of crystal alchemy singing bowls, my entire body vibrated in recognition. I began to cry. The beauty and frequency of the instruments called out to me. Deep within, I felt them murmur to me, "We found you, you are home now, and you are loved."

Sitting at the hospital bed holding my mom's hand, I realized that I never shared my recent accomplishments with her, nor the joy and love I had developed for my crystal alchemy bowls. I wondered if she would have been happy with the changes I made to my life and would have enjoyed seeing me play my bowls. It saddened me, knowing that I would never really know how she felt about any of this or how much I had changed as an individual. In the undercurrent of this sadness, it dawned on me that I did not share specific details of my life with her as a coping mechanism to guard my heart. The pain of our past had affected my ability to share in the present.

Returning to my hotel room that night, I leaned into all the tools I had learned over the past few years of my awakening. I chose not to numb out and instead to stay in my heart, allowing the sounds and vibrations of the crystal alchemy bowls to soothe my soul. With the sound bowls, it was as if my heart was being massaged. I showed up to my yoga mat (a white hotel towel) with Yoga with Adriene, listened to my meditation teacher, Davidji, on Insight Timer, and meditated. I drank green juice and walked to the hospital doing Breathwork. I cared for my body, mind, and soul so that I could be fully present with my mom at her hospital bedside.

After the first 24 hours, it was clear that my mom's heart was too damaged to pump on its own. She would never wake up. My mother was dying, and the grief of losing someone else was beginning to well up. It felt too much to lose my mother, too. Within the last six months, my "Pop" had died from cancer, and my mother-in-law passed away unexpectedly.

Even as I steeled myself for what was coming, I needed support. I reached out to a friend and asked, "What should I do?"

"Tell her it's okay to move on," she told me.

My heart broke again, and my mind screamed, "NO! PLEASE, not another death."

But there was nothing else to do except surrender.

On my mother's last day, I was blessed with an "earth angel." The room's vibration had completely changed when I arrived at the hospital. Music played softly, the fluorescent lights turned off, and the window blinds lifted, revealing a cloudy sky with the sun peeking through and a ray streaming down as if to say, "You are not alone."

"I hope it's okay," the nurse said, "I felt like your mom wanted some music and natural light."

She paused, looked me in the eyes, handed me two crystals, and said, "She doesn't have much time."

With tears rolling down my face, I replied with a sob caught in my throat, "Thank you."

During her final moments, I played "Hearing with Our Hearts," a song with crystal alchemy bowls by Jeralyn Glass. As the music played for the third time, I stood by her bed and visualized the vibrations of the sounds soothing her body and guiding her soul home. I kissed her forehead, held her hand, and whispered in her ear, "I love you Mama. It's okay to let go. May you be at peace." And with that, she flatlined.

With a lump in my throat and tears streaming down my face, I thought to myself, *I never shared my dreams, I kept my heart closed for fear of being hurt again. I am so sorry, Mama.*

As I tuned into the lingering sounds of the bowls, I suddenly felt a wave of gratitude wash over me as I realized what a beautiful gift I was given—time to say goodbye and help her transition with the healing vibrations of love and sacred sound. With tears continuing to flow down my face, I smiled as my heart filled with an abundance of love and gratitude.

Today is her birthday. I am here at the beach, looking at the water, witnessing the curiosity of walking into the ocean and leaving this world. I recognize that this was not an actual desire to die, but rather an opportunity to choose how to live— what to let go of, how to feel, and what next step is mine to take.

By embracing my loss, my journey, and my transformation with grief, I recognize now that grief is love. They are intertwined. There is no "one way" to grieve; we all have our own process. Grief is an opportunity to allow emotions to arise, breathe them, accept them, and transform them into love.

Returning home, stepping into the room with my alchemy bowls, the accumulated grief and loss breaks my heart open and I collapse on the ground, sobbing uncontrollably. Suddenly through my sobs, I hear the alchemy bowls playing. I fall silent, pushing myself up, tears streaming down, checking to see if I was imagining it, but no— *they are singing!*

The vibrations of my pain and tears were making them sing, this vibration of love. I laid back down and allowed all my feelings, emotions, and sensations to arise, and with the vibrations and sounds of the bowls, I felt my heart opening, transmuting the pain to love. Showing me that, in the end, grief is simply love.

WORKSHEET: ANOTHER STEP ON YOUR SPIRAL PATH

OFFERED BY ROXANNA FIGUEROA

How can we explore and transform grief with new perspectives and new understanding?

Here are some strategies for being present with grief, honoring the pain, and beginning to lean into love and healing your heart.

Step 1: Allow

The arrival of grief reminds us of the undeniable reality of our interconnectedness to all of life and love. It becomes a sacred place when we allow ourselves the courage and space to be present with all the accompanying emotions, thoughts, feelings, and sensations—witnessing them as they move through us and holding ourselves with kindness and compassion.

Exercise: Take a moment to close your eyes. Take three deep breaths in and out of your nose. Relax your jaw, relax your shoulders, relax your stomach. Place one hand on your heart and ask yourself the following:

How am I feeling (leave the story behind, feel into the feelings)?
What do I need right now?

Now feel your heart and imagine light pouring in from the crown of your head into your heart, soothing the pain.

Take another deep breath and open your eyes.

Journal: I invite you to journal about your experience.

_____

_____

_____

Step 2: Express

Acknowledge and express your emotions in creative, healthy ways through music, dance, art, journaling, and outlets that allow you to work through the mixture of emotions while being fully present with them, as much or as little as you can—holding them with love and light.

Please go to the link below for resources and Spotify playlists.

Step 3: Compassion and Connection

Be patient, loving, and kind to yourself. Surround yourself with supportive friends, grief support groups, or a mental health practitioner.

Journal: What is one thing that brings you comfort?

_____

_____

_____

Step 4: Healing with Crystal Alchemy Singing Bowls

Alchemy bowls create a different healing experience compared to plain quartz bowls as they are infused with gemstones, precious metals, minerals, and earth substances. Our bodies are crystalline in structure and thus able to absorb the quartz sounds. Through sound, vibration, and intention, these frequencies can help instill deep relaxation, create balance, and elicit an overall sense of well-being.

Please go to the link below for a free crystal alchemy sound healing bath.
Resources: linktr.ee/attuningwithin.

ROXANNA FIGUEROA

Roxanna Figueroa is a trusted guide to those ready to say yes to their inner transformation and awaken to their wholeness. Working with individuals on their healing journey and fellow practitioners stepping into their brilliance, she provides a sacred space bringing compassion and deep presence. She uses various modalities, including Sound, traditional Japanese Reiki, Meditation, Embodiment, and Functional Medicine Coaching, to promote the full spectrum of healing.

With a Bachelor's in Psychology and a minor in Ethnic Studies, her professional career has encompassed working at various heart-centered non-profit organizations whose missions entailed supporting people with cancer and end-of-life transitions; promoting racial, economic, and gender justice, and advancing the welfare of animals.

It has been a journey of surrender and lifelong devotion to growth, service, and discovery that has brought her here today as an intuitive healing practitioner and author.

https://linktr.ee/attuningwithin

HOW I FAILED ONE BOY

NICOLE FABIAN

Sixteen years into my teaching career, I received a phone call from one of my best friends. As I picked up the phone, I heard, "Nicole, we lost our Anthony."

I heard one other word: Overdose.

The air in my lungs was sucked out of my body. I dropped to my knees, next to the phone, in my empty classroom. I don't remember much more from that phone call besides how hollow the room felt. It was like being encapsulated in an echo chamber, no sound, no movement, just a fragment of time that stood still and branded into my memory.

From that singular and significant moment, my teaching career would never feel or be the same.

The call to be a teacher came to me when I was just eleven years old.

My 6th grade classmates and I were given the opportunity to volunteer in a classroom with students that had experienced traumatic brain injuries (TBI). It was the first time I worked with anyone who had a disability, but that didn't stop us from playing basketball, making crafts, filling the vending machines, and counting quarters. Those kids expanded my heart and showed me I could become comfortable with the uncomfortable.

That knowing brought me another message: "Nicole, you will teach."

From a young age, I had always felt the presence of God, spirit, angels and other light beings, but I wasn't encouraged to share what I saw, felt, or heard. Sometimes, it actually frightened me, so I kept it mostly to myself. But, this message from the higher realms or a higher being of consciousness came with a truth I couldn't deny. This calling landed in my heart and bones, and I began my journey to being a teacher.

It was a turbulent path, with numerous personal battles to win through high school and college. But I always felt as if I was protected, led, and guided by my spiritual team. I used what I learned to become a teacher full of experiences, traumas, and celebrations that would help me better connect to my students.

Over time, I came to understand that I wanted to use my gifts and intuition to help my students in ways I needed when I was a child.

I purposely worked with what some would say were the most challenging groups of students. These were students placed in a behavior management classroom and were given labels such as Emotionally Disturbed, ADHD and Other Health Impaired. I looked at it as an opportunity to support the students who needed the most love and acceptance. The labels given to my students didn't capture the reasons behind the behavior. Many of my students struggled with trauma, depression, dysregulated nervous systems, and sensory disorders. The traditional school setting exasperated their symptoms.

They desired an alternative way to learn, and I loved the challenge of proving to my students that I cared for them and that my classroom was a safe place. A safe place to learn and to show their true and authentic selves. They were able to express their emotions and voice their struggles. I created a classroom that when people walked in, they were inclined to say, "I love how it feels in here," and that brought me so much joy.

Although most people thought I had the toughest job in the building, I felt it was the most rewarding and best job in the world.

Ten years into teaching, Anthony came into my life. He was a high school freshman who didn't have any significant behavior issues, but faced some difficulty with fitting in socially.

Here he was, this smart kid with a huge pile of books that he refused to put in his locker. I can still see him carrying these books with him from class to class. His affection for reading is something his family and I continue to treasure as one of our fondest memories.

Anthony did great academically. He was bright and had a strong desire to learn. I remember him being so successful with the behavior management program that another teacher encouraged me and the team to move him into a less restrictive environment at the end of the year.

I had some concerns about how he might fare socially, but there wasn't data to support keeping him with us. He had great grades, good behavior, and steady attendance. To this day, the word data sits like a sour bubble in my throat when I say it. The question of why data was more important than following my intuition and gut feeling of what a student really needed will cast a shadow over my grief and make me doubt myself, my teaching abilities, and the entire educational system for years to come.

I wouldn't work with Anthony again until his senior year of high school.

Divine timing put us back together. I was at my friend Jeanne's house sitting in her hot tub with her twin sister, June. June mentioned to me that she was dating Anthony's father, and that Anthony was really struggling with school. I casually suggested that his parents schedule a meeting to see if we could get him back into the program. A few weeks later, Anthony was my student again.

Anthony had changed some since I last saw him. He was now a talented wrestler, a smart kid who still got bored easily with the academics, and *wow!* could he see right through you if you were inauthentic. His humor was spot-on, often hysterical, but sometimes a bit hurtful.

Our goal was to make sure Anthony would graduate on time. His family and I rallied around him to help him get the credits he needed. I took my job super seriously, and I went to battle for my students to ensure they would graduate. We had difficult and intense meetings. My clumsiness ended up being a way to lighten the mood. Who would have ever guessed that me tipping over in a chair during a meeting or falling into potted plants as we walked through the school's atrium would be memories Anthony's parents and I still laugh about today?

Anthony saw things the way they were, and, at times, this world was a painful and difficult place for him. Anthony, like many of us, found ways to numb his pain. He caused us a lot of worries, but he made it through his senior year. He allowed us to love him and guide him just enough to help him get through.

Anthony and I saw each other a few times after graduation, at his dad's and June's wedding, at a local hockey game, and some other family gatherings. From the outside looking in, it was obvious to me he was hurting and his battle with addiction was evident. I prayed that he would understand and know his own kind and loving soul, and that he would see that he had so many beautiful gifts to share. Regretfully, I never said any of these things to him while he was alive. I feared overstepping boundaries now that he was no longer in my classroom.

After his death, I started to question everything I had done as his teacher.

He was successful his freshman year, and then we let him go. Was the gap of time between the end of his freshman year and the beginning of his senior year too long? With the lack of support during that time and after graduation did he find himself overwhelmed and alone?

He was such a smart kid, but that wasn't enough, I thought. The school system failed him. I failed him, too.

Anthony was a highly sensitive kid.

I'll forever ask myself, *why didn't we have more in place to help him deal with his emotions and feelings?*

Why do we not help our students connect to themselves emotionally, physically, spiritually as well as academically?

Why did we not help him learn to self-regulate his emotions, learn to repair, expand, and restore his nervous system?

Why didn't we teach him that drugs and alcohol can numb out the pain but there are other ways to get through without harming our bodies?

Anthony died. I lost him. I didn't save him. I felt I could save all my students. My gifts as his teacher did not impact him in the superhero way I thought was possible. I thought all I needed to do was love them and give them a safe place to learn. They needed more from the system and from me.

I no longer felt I was doing what I was called to do.

Shortly after his death, Anthony began to come to me in dreams and in visions. He encouraged me to open up my senses and dive into sharing my intuitive gifts. I wasn't sure what he meant; I hadn't explored or even recognized my intuitive gifts since I was a teen. I knew they were there and I knew I had them, but I never felt comfortable talking about or sharing them. It was scary to think of sharing with others that I could talk to their loved ones who had passed, or tell someone that I could check in with their guides to assure them that everything will be okay. What would people think?

Anthony would come in as clear as could be. I could even sometimes hear and feel him next to me when I was awake. Overwhelmed with the feeling that I had let him down, I begged him for forgiveness and he assured me that his path was his to follow and there was nothing to forgive. He explained he was here now to encourage me to follow my path and share the divine gifts given to me.

I don't know if I will ever let myself off the hook as Anthony encourages me to do. It still feels better to me to hold onto a part of the responsibility. In a way, it's like holding onto a piece of him.

Anthony still comes to me years later, guiding me, alongside other members of my spiritual team, as I navigate my path on this planet.

One time, his spirit came forward to me on a subway in New

York City. The train was filled with armed service members for a
Veteran's Day parade. I was thanking the people dressed in military
uniforms for their service when I heard Anthony boldly say, "My
dad would love this shit!" He made me laugh out loud. I'm still
friends with his dad, and Anthony's amusing remark is spot on.

Anthony is the same in spirit as in human form. Full of humor,
raw dialogue with no filter, with his brazen "I am who I am, take it
or leave it" attitude. It's comforting.

I am not sure exactly what led him down the path of addiction
but I do know it was his way of numbing some sort of underlying
pain. The root or reason is less important now. I believe all behavior
has meaning, and we can still support and heal without knowing or
understanding all the details.

In my grief, I asked to leave my behavior management
classroom and teach our self-contained class for autism. I didn't feel
as if I was worthy of teaching my students anymore. What if I
continued to let them down? Maybe if I worked with a different
group of students, my pain would subside.

My new group of students had a lot of Anthony's highly
sensitive qualities. There was no bullshitting anyone in this
classroom. I worked quickly to learn how to support my students
and their individual needs, and, in return, my students gave me a
beautiful and safe place to teach.

Outside of school, I dove into discovering my spiritual gifts. I
learned how to give intuitive readings. I started my own business
consulting with families on how to support their struggling children.
I learned about human design, astrology, repairing the nervous
system, and I became a Reiki practitioner. I learned self-care
practices that served me and my students, and started to develop
booklets and courses to support neurodiverse individuals and highly
intuitive and sensitive beings.

I am beginning the next chapter.

I am gently weaning myself towards leaving the education
system. It doesn't align with me and my calling anymore. After
Anthony died, I lost the call to teach in the institution of education.

Sometimes, the fear of leaving teaching paralyzes me. I've

clenched hard to the person I thought I was and to the idea that I was going to have a thirty-year journey in education. I have always identified as a teacher.

My guides and angels, including Anthony, get frustrated with me. I get a vision of them shaking their heads and taking deep exasperated breaths. They tell me, "This is not the end of teaching. You are a teacher, you always will be a teacher. You have bigger and greater things to do." They tell me greater things will come once I take the leap.

One day, as if to confirm that, I received an unexpected message during an online meditation class. As I was sitting in silence after a beautiful sound bath, a clear message came forward. Spirit said to my soul, "It's time to move forward. Let go of the rope. Release. Surrender. Trust."

This has become my mantra.

When will I be ready to let go and take the leap? I am not sure. What I do know is that each step I take in trusting myself and surrendering to the fear of letting go will lead me to teaching others along the way.

I see Anthony looking at me with his feet up on a desk and his hands cradling the back of his head, with a discerning smile, as I write this, so I must be on the right track.

WORKSHEET: ANOTHER STEP ON YOUR SPIRAL PATH

OFFERED BY NICOLE FABIAN

D o you feel yourself as a highly sensitive or intuitive being? If so, here are a few helpful and supportive tips to help you shine brighter.

I. Organizing/Decluttering.

Clearing space allows light in, releases old energy, and allows in new vitality.

Where in your life do you have a space that needs to be cleared? Start with one small space at a time. For example: I love getting my car organized and clean because it is easier to manage than my home. Once I conquer that, I move onto drawers, closets, and rooms in my home.

What space would you like to start with?

_____

_____

_____

II. Knowing your child/self through the lens of:

Astrology
Numerology
Enneagram
Human Design

Diving into any of these categories will give you insight on how you work. I have learned so much about myself by looking at my charts. The more I know about myself and learn to love the way I am, the better I am for myself and others. Have fun exploring your own charts by starting with this simple question.

What is your date, time, and place of birth?

_____

_____

_____

III. Working with your nervous system.

Learning to work and repair my nervous system has had a huge impact on my growth and healing. Being able to understand how our nervous system responds helps us heal and grow.

When you are asked to do deep breathing exercises do you feel like you calm down or become more anxious?

_____

_____

_____

Everyone responds uniquely and it is important to learn what strategies and tools work for you.

IV. Setting up rituals and procedures

Rituals help a highly sensitive person protect their energy and support their mind, body, and soul. Meditating in the morning allows me to connect to my guides and set up an intention that will lead me through the day. Clearing the energy I have picked up throughout the day with an epsom salt bath in the evening helps me get back to myself and sleep better.

How do you set up your day to incorporate rituals and routines that enhance your experience and support you?

_____

_____

_____

What is one daily routine that you have in place that you feel supports you at the beginning or end of the day?

_____

_____

_____

V. Gifting yourself self-love and celebrating along the path

This is the most important step: finding love, joy, and celebration along the way. Healing and expanding is not easy, and we can get caught up in how hard it is. It is important to step back and celebrate how far you have come and to find a way to honor and love yourself.

What is one thing you can celebrate right now?

_____

_____

_____

Resources: linktr.ee/nicolefabian

NICOLE FABIAN

Nicole Fabian was born and raised in Rochester, New York. She has been a Special Education Teacher for more than twenty years, following a calling she received at the young age of eleven years old.

More recently, Nicole has served as a Behavior and Intuitive Consultant. Her life's work has been to create safe learning environments that embrace the whole child. Nicole's intuition and spirituality has led her through life, and her desire to reach more people inspired her to start her own business as an intuitive, educational consultant, and family coach.

Trusting and working with her intuition has helped her navigate the most challenging circumstances, and she has been guided to offer others support through her intuitive readings and Reiki sessions. Nicole's expertise and intuition help individuals, families, and teachers find peace and healing in their homes, in the school setting, within their careers, relationships, and, most importantly, within themselves.

linktr.ee/nicolefabian

PARADIGM SHIFT: MY NEURO-ATYPICAL JOURNEY OF SELF-AWARENESS

WENDY PETERMAN, PH.D.

My sixteen-year-old daughter called me from a Roman archaeological site in England.

She chattered excitedly, "I was listening to a professor talk about patterns in Roman architecture, and I blurted, 'It's a Fibonacci sequence!' He looked stunned, then eventually said, 'Yes. I never thought about it that way. I guess it is a Fibonacci sequence.' I wish I had the tool I made for measuring the golden ratio so I could show that the architecture demonstrates the Fibonacci effect."

Listening to her enthusiasm about the golden ratio and Roman architecture, I was reminded of the challenges in homeschooling her.

Having quickly worked her way through every math book offered, at the age of ten she demanded all math lessons be written in Roman numerals. I did my best to keep her engaged with math in a way that related to real life while also meeting the state standards for her grade level. Getting it wrong could have resulted in the dreaded response I knew too well, "No. It's not interesting to me. I'm not doing it." After all, my avid dedication to homeschooling stemmed from my own under-stimulating experiences with traditional schools.

Returning to the phone call about the research expedition, she added, "It's weird that the archaeologists have no clue what kind of soil we're digging in. It seems like that would be important to know. I mean, I was digging on my site, and I noticed a lot of clay in the layer I'm uncovering. So, I took it over to the lead researcher and asked what kind of soil it was. He said, 'Ummmm…yellow?' The yellow means something about the chemistry of that period, doesn't it?"

Laughter and pride welled up in me as I recalled scenes of my days as a soil science graduate student, taking my daughter as my field assistant to explore the soils of Oregon. We climbed the cut banks of roads in the rainy Coast Range to identify the details of ancient soils.

She teased out a crumbly black piece, and said, "Mom, this looks like charcoal."

"Yes. I do see a layer of charcoal in this soil profile," I acknowledged. "Why do you think that might be there?"

Looking at the trees above and the broken black line in the soil, she guessed, "It shows where there was a wildfire in the past?"

Years later, this exact moment will arise in my mind as I listen to a scientist talk about the challenge of identifying the timeframe of wildfires in areas where all trees have burned. Without some trees or stumps, they can't use burn scars or tree rings to estimate when past fires occurred.

"You might use charcoal in the soil profile along with carbon or hydrogen isotopes to find the fire history in severely burned forests," I remarked, seeing in my mind a hologram of the trees, the fire, and the soil with its charred surface and intact roots. Mentally turning the image in various directions to see the interactions of the components, I offered, "If you look at the details of how the soil burn severity classes are defined, you will be able to see a more holistic picture of how the post-fire soil conditions relate to forest recovery in your study plots."

This unstructured, holographic way of thinking is the result of my neuro-uniqueness, otherwise known as Autism Spectrum Disorder.

People usually don't believe I am on the autism spectrum. "You're too friendly," they say. Or, "Autistics don't have empathy like you do." Those who do believe me say, "I would never be able to tell." My usual response is, "That's because you don't understand autism."

The truth is: My autism isn't about your experience of me. It's about my experience of me.

It's common for women on the autism spectrum to evade diagnosis by camouflaging as neurotypical people whose brains function in ways considered typical within their culture. In fact, "camouflage exhaustion" is becoming a pandemic for adult female autistics.

Only by looking back at our childhoods can signs of autism be identified.

To me, childhood was characterized by a rich fantasy life. My mind was always full of pictures. My body effervesced with intense feelings like joy, fascination, and curiosity, especially in nature. I could read fluently and do basic math problems before entering kindergarten just from hanging out with books and my parents.

I thought my vivid, deeply immersive experience of life was normal.

It's only when I started to hear the reactions of the adults in my world that I learned I was anything but normal, and they had worn themselves out trying to make me so.

Frustrated, one teacher took me to the library, showed me the magical bookshelves, and gave me a special pass to come to the library any time I wanted. I loved this teacher, so I was shocked to read her comments on my report cards. "Wendy is very socially backward and does not engage with other children."

My second grade teacher reported I didn't speak for the first six months of the school year.

And, my mom loves to tell a story about how in first grade, I was in an advanced math class, but very remedial in reading. They put me in the lowest reading group, and I daydreamed and didn't engage. They gave me extra phonics lessons and special reading help. Although I loved the reading tutors, I never improved at reading aloud. When my mom suggested they move me into the highest reading group they finally, reluctantly, gave me a "social promotion" so I could be with other girls my age. Once I found a class stimulating, I came alive and excelled at reading. When I graduated high school with honors, my first-grade teacher said she would never forget how I went from floundering to flourishing just by being offered a real challenge.

We moved often, and new teachers had the same misconceptions. I ended up in libraries teaching myself math everywhere we went. No teacher ever knew that at the age of ten, I could do my dad's calculus homework and read my mom's microbiology textbook aloud.

My sister called me an "idiot savant." She explained it was someone who seemed unintelligent but was a mathematical genius. Despite its popularity in the media, savant-ism is rare, even among autistics. Oddly, math is uninteresting to me unless it's describing something fascinating like saturated water flow in a soil matrix or pressure differentials that make water flow upward in trees.

By my freshman year of college, I realized that rather than spending time in classrooms hearing lectures about all the things teachers had been saying on repeat for many years, I wanted to spend my time in nature, hiking and teaching children about organic gardening. I realized that being me wasn't about following the strict rules of what I had been told to be. It was about pursuing ideas to the edges of existence for the sheer love of knowing, regardless of whether or not it's comfortable for others.

Being me was about embodying the wonder and awe of tiny moments of intense focus, in which the details of the infinite universe echo, creating holograms in my mind.

Also, being me was incredibly lonely. I often described it as a "deep well of loneliness." I felt like an alien, like I actually did not belong on this planet.

It wasn't until I was researching autism to support one of my adopted children that I understood my own experience of hypersensitivity and alienation. This awareness brought to light why I—and my feelings and sensations—are so intense, why my thoughts arrive in massive onslaughts of mental pictures, and why the world seems to be made for everyone but me.

I started to see myself as a person with disabilities and superpowers. I noticed that leaning in to my special interests gave me the courage to overcome my challenges to function well in my chosen profession. The desire to do well in soil science and tree physiology motivated me to study self-regulation skills like meditation and yoga, and communication skills like deep listening and compassionate communication.

In leadership training for the Forest Service, I learned about the three ingredients of emotional intelligence: self-regulation, other-awareness, and self-awareness.

"Self-regulation" can include any tools I need to calm my physiology from "stimming" (behaviors like stroking, rocking, or pacing), to forest bathing, to time in the "Quiet Room."

"Other-awareness" includes my natural deep empathy but also tools that help me categorize behaviors to understand how people would like information to be given to them.

"Self-awareness" is not just knowing I need to be careful not to interrupt others or talk incessantly when I'm feeling exuberant about a topic. It's also knowing I have talents in deeply learning about things that interest me, and sharing that learning when it is relevant to people who need advice or a different perspective. Offering a different perspective is, after all, one of my beloved superpowers. And nothing gives me more fulfillment than the moments when I can share wisdom and insight with my own children.

I recently celebrated my fiftieth birthday with my daughter, now an adult completing her Ph.D. in sociology.

The night before we flew to meet each other in New York City, she texted me, "Hey, will you help me craft my corporate research proposal while we're together? You're a nerdy person, so I figured it would be a fun activity for you," she said.

"Sure. I'd love to," I replied. Of course, I'd love to! I squealed and ran into my partner's office to chatter incessantly about the wonderful time we would have dreaming up her research proposal.

The next day, sitting at the desk in our hotel room, she laid out three different pathways of thought she could use to develop her research questions. Inquiring about the audience, the data, and the technology available to her, I formed a holographic image in my mind, gradually adding the details of her social networking approach to qualitative data analysis. "I see how these three pathways inter-relate," I said. "You could propose each as a separate idea or all three as layers of complexity to pursue the questions progressively."

"Oh right! I could lay the groundwork with the basic question, then point out how that would lead to the next question, which then could be used with this other technology to take it all the way to the heart of a complex issue," she said, seeing how my hologram transformed into a sequential line of reason. "Thanks. Now go entertain yourself while I write this up."

Laying back on the bed, I reflected on how far we've come... how far *I've* come.

I can see how my years as a mother and soil scientist have shown me I am empathetic, resilient, and respected. My unstructured way of thinking makes me creative, and my depth of emotion makes me strong.

Every day I gain perspective by adding new details to the hologram.

Every year I grow in the reassurance of arriving at a new phase of life without fear that I am not enough or that I do not belong.

I am enough and I do belong, and I love my neuro-atypical brain.

WORKSHEET: ANOTHER STEP ON YOUR SPIRAL PATH

OFFERED BY WENDY PETERMAN, PH.D.

For me, nature is where I feel connected and at peace. When I feel overwhelmed, disconnected, or dysregulated, I can go outside and breathe the fresh air, feel the breeze on my face, and tune in to the tiny details of the natural world.

In nature, I feel like I belong. My brain can work out confusing human social interactions in the background as I wander in the woods, calming my nervous system and feeling included by the trees, rocks, and critters of the woods.

I have created a ten-minute guided meditation for connecting with nature. It can be done anywhere, and it would be nice to do it outside. Please use this link to access my Forests of the Soul Nature Meditation on YouTube.com: youtu.be/Qk1VYmXWMtI

Or, follow along with these written instructions.

Make yourself comfortable, in contact with a supportive surface.

Call attention to your breath, breathing normally.

Call attention to your spine—the base of your spine supporting your body, the top of your head and the space beyond you.

Call your attention to the sensation of gravity and the effect it has on your body, and the contact between your body and the surface beneath it.

Relax into gravity.

Imagine your body forming roots that connect down into the earth.

Feel the connection between your body and the earth.

If you're outside, you can notice a feeling of air on your skin, the smells around you. Maybe there is some fresh soil, some cut grass, some decaying leaves.

If you're inside, just imagine those things. Imagine you can smell fresh air, plants, the ground.

Those things emit chemicals that stimulate happiness, chemicals in our bodies.

Breathe those in, and let your body release the positive chemicals.

Imagine you can see the sky, the blue, gray, white, pink, purple, colors of the sky.

You might express some gratitude and appreciation:

"Thank you, sky, you're beautiful. I value and appreciate you."

Imagine around you there are trees, rocks, and notice things about them—stems, bark, leaves, needles, smooth surfaces, bugs, snails—all going about their business, naturally connected to the earth.

Imagine you can hear a stream.

Feel that sound, constant, flowing over rocks, pebbles, and sand…to get to where you are and be present in this moment with that exact sound.

With this sense of peace, presence, connection with the earth and the natural world, open your eyes.

Begin to move around, and slowly come back into your day, feeling refreshed, uplifted, and at peace.

WENDY PETERMAN, PH.D.

Wendy Peterman, Ph.D., identifies as a visual/pattern-oriented autistic with selective mutism tendencies. She helps neuro-diverse women experiencing overwhelm or masking-fatigue to relax and feel a sense of belonging through connecting with nature.

She holds a B.A. in Dance, an M.S. in Soil Science, and a Ph.D. in Forest Engineering. She believes that true resilience for ecological systems, including humans, comes from working with their natural processes and innate potential.

In addition to her professional life, Dr. Peterman has led a full personal life raising one biological child and four adopted children. She spends her free time hiking, quilting, and woodworking.

Videos of her outdoor adventures can be seen on YouTube at forestsofthesoul.

linktr.ee/wendybrddance

FROM LIFE'S FIRE TO LIFE'S GIFTS

KATHY GATES

When the sun sets in the desert, the night sky comes alive. I can almost touch the blanket of stars as it unfolds over me. I breathe in the cool darkness of the night. There is a special energy here.

My ancestors are close.

A tribal fire burns, and a chant fills my ears, "Earth - My body; Water - My Blood; Air - My breath, and Fire - My Spirit," crying out as 200 women gather and the smell of charred wood and smoke rise up into the starry night.

My heart pounds so loudly in my chest that it reverberates into my ears. I close my eyes tightly to try to take it all in. As I open them and look out, the 1,200-degree burning bits of orange fire lay glowing in the dark night. Scattered before me in a ten-foot-long walkway, I can feel the heat from the pathway on my skin, it warms my face. My mind races.

I read that people come to fire walks for all kinds of reasons. Most of them, to walk away from something and to walk towards something.

What am I walking away from?

What am I walking toward?

Can I even do this?

I breathe a slow deep breath. My body calms. I feel my Soul answer with a resounding "Yes! You Must Do This."

I stand there for a moment and lean into this new feeling emerging within me. This clarity. Yes, I need to do this. I need to shed all this emotional baggage. Let it burn away. Feed it to the fire.

My body and mind flood with stories, moments, burdens, and emotions that weighed me down. I could feel them all rising up inside of me, ready to offer themselves to the fire.

But, wait! Like the lash of a whip, my thinking brain kicks on.

What am I doing?

Am I really going to do this?

What if I get burned?

What would I tell people?... Oh, I thought I could walk across hot coals??

I hear my mother's voice say, "Surely, you are smarter than that."

Am I?

I breathe a long, ragged breath.

My mind rewinds a few months back to the summer.

"My stomach has been really bothering me lately," my dad said. What felt like a moment later, we were discussing if chemotherapy was worth the misery it caused. He ultimately decided that it was not, and he chose to spend his remaining time being with the family he loved.

The next four months between his diagnosis and his death was a swirl of fear, worry, heartache, and great love. He allowed me to experience some of the greatest moments of love I have ever known. He was this wonderful combination of strength, wit, and gentleness.

Standing at the fire's edge, I ache to hear his voice again or see him smile. I've not had time to process this huge loss and still can't adequately put it into words. But my body knows the toll it has taken.

While I watched my beloved father succumb to cancer, my own marriage was falling apart. My husband's addiction had careened out of control and the lies spiraled in my mind. I never knew what I was going to find when I came home, and I was certain that one day I would find him dead from an overdose.

Driving back and forth between my parents' home and mine, my emotions were all over the place. I would leave my dad's bedside where my dad refused pain meds because he wanted to stay awake for whatever time he could have with his girls. I would then come home to a perfectly healthy man, who was passed out on pain meds because being awake and living was just too much for him. I used to pray, "Lord, help me get through these days."

I couldn't bring up the addiction when there was so little time left with my dad! But my heart knew I needed to do something about it. For the past three years, I had tried everything I knew of to help my husband. I maxed out all of my resources as a trauma therapist and phoned in favors from most of my therapist friends. I was becoming more desperate, and we were falling more behind on our bills as he continued to lose jobs.

I'm not sure if it was courage or a feeling of total defeat that motivated me, but one month after my dad died, I asked my husband to move out and I filed for a divorce.

With that choice made, my mind wandered to the next likely question, "Now what?"

Somewhere, just out of ear shot, an inner fire was quietly calling me. My body was begging for me to lay down my burdens as I felt my ancestors weaving their sacred song into the fabric of my Soul.

I struggled to let go of the defenses that I had outgrown, but somewhere deep inside, the urgency for a grand gesture, a sacred ritual, began to form and I started to listen.

While all this grief swirled around me like a whirlwind, I oddly found myself in a place of feeling like I had nothing to lose. That thought liberated and motivated me to stretch outside of my comfort zone. If I had learned anything from my father's death, it was that life was way too short not to enjoy it. I realized that I had stopped living and was merely existing. That realization shook me to the core.

I decided to quit my job, and I stepped out onto the shaky unknown territory of entrepreneurship. I poured all my energy into starting a holistic trauma center. I had been planning, dreaming, scheming, and calling this into existence for years, but never had the right time or support to pursue my dreams.

But a new fire was already aflame deep within me and couldn't be ignored.

As I approached my forty-ninth birthday, my Soul scribbled an idea into my brain that wove its way into my heart.

I needed self-care, Soul-care. I declared the time between my forty-ninth and fiftieth birthdays to be "The Year of Kathy," where my sole purpose would be grounded in the business of intensive self-care. There was a tingling of delight in my Spirit when I said yes to this invitation.

I knew the very first place I needed to go: the ocean. I packed up my car with minimal supplies and headed to a beach bungalow belonging to a friend of a friend.

Ahhh… just hearing the waves and feeling the warm ocean breeze immediately soothed some of the heaviness like a salve to my Soul. I spent most mornings walking along the beach, burying my feet deep into the soft cool sand and feeling the tension melt off my shoulders.

I was often joined by my father's presence. We strolled along picking up seashells, as fond memories from my childhood replayed in my mind. We talked. I cried. I said thank you. I slept.

His presence was a recurring theme throughout that year of healing. Although he was never really far away, there were spots and moments where his energy was so palpable. I expected to look over and see him.

My dad loved to go out West and hunt. Long ago, he showed me pictures of his trips, telling me that the camera couldn't even begin to capture how beautiful and magnificent the mountains were and that someday he wanted to take us there to see this beauty with our own eyes. That year, in The Year of Kathy, I visited seven National Parks, and I felt him with me often and could hear his voice telling me about the elk or the wonders of the mountains.

At one spot, I felt his presence so strongly, I had to pull over and call my sister. We cried together on the phone as we both knew how much he loved Nature and the sacredness of it. I brought my adult son with me to a few of the parks. We shared memories of dad, and we made new memories between us.

The more experiences I had like these, the more I wanted. This freedom was only possible when I was willing to step out of my comfort zone and lean heavily on the Universe and trust her to carry me through.

So here I am. Can I trust her?

Standing at the edge of that fire walk, I hear my heart say, "Hell yes! I can trust her!" She had been orchestrating every step. Every cell in my body resonated this truth.

Women line either side of the walkway cheering, chanting their support and commitment to light it all on fire. The whole thing was otherworldly. One of the coolest things about the Universe is the sisterhood that is created among women who barely know each other but are bonded together with a familiar experience. Exhaustion, self-care, recovery…all of these are too familiar to too many women, and many of them were here to burn that heaviness away, too.

Two women I connected with earlier yell out to me personally, "Go Queen Kathy!! You got this! Give it all to the fire!"

I intend to do exactly that as my foot steps onto the searing red hot coals. My mind goes quiet, blown away by the experience, humbled and in awe of the power of the fire.

As the heat rises up from the fire, my energy soars and the fear is replaced with an exuberant joy. My confidence skyrockets as I continue to put one foot in front of the other, offering the fire a kiss with each foot. I feel so alive and unstoppable.

A group of women wait at the finish line to celebrate my journey through the fire and hug me. I step off the coals feeling bigger than life, bolder than I had ever dreamed, and, literally, vibrating with life energy.

We cheer and squeal with delight as we witness each other transforming. I immediately get back in line and walk three times across the fire that night. Each time, a deeper purification as my body continues to give all of the weight it has been carrying to the fire and begins to harness her power.

We gather around the campfire and stay up talking into the night. Our bodies buzz with life. When I finally return to my room, I lay my head on the pillow. A big smile crosses my face, proud and thrilled to have stepped through the flames and into a new chapter of being.

The next morning, I meet my new friends for breakfast and a hike up a mountain to a Buddhist temple. Prayer flags line the steep path. I reflect on what happened the night before. I had liberated a new version of me that was so grounded and humbled and yet so powerful and alive.

Climbing, I recite a blessing with each step. I still feel the power of the fire roaring within me. Every step is filled with a word of gratitude.

When I reach the temple, my gratitude fills all of me. Receiving this gift, I write in the sand some of the things I gave to the fire: Fear, overwhelm, shame, worry, helplessness. I know I had totally released them and severed the energetic chords of those contracts. I ask the wind to scatter those cut cords far from me.

Walking down the mountain, I am a new woman. I claim what the fire gave me: Power. Courage. Connectedness. Truth. But mostly, I claim love...love for myself and the woman I am happy to be.

WORKSHEET: ANOTHER STEP ON YOUR SPIRAL PATH

OFFERED BY KATHY GATES

Take a few minutes and do an inventory of your emotional self-care.

What feels like it is in balance, and what old patterns do you keep running into? Notice areas like body image/health, finances, relationships with others, relationship with self, career, family, fun, and pleasure.

_____

_____

_____

What are your beliefs and what patterns do you often find yourself in around these areas of life? As you gain clarity about the status of your emotional health, be willing to be curious as you discover patterns and reserve judgment. If you notice that you are beating

yourself up or criticizing yourself, put that on your list as a pattern
you want to move away from.

_____

_____

_____

Looking over your lists, begin to feel into the ways your body is
holding these painful limited beliefs.

Gauge what percentage of this energy IS NOT useful to where
you want to go and what percentage IS serving you.

Sometimes this can look like:

I love that I am independent, but sometimes I'm too
independent and I push others away, or I have a difficult time
trusting others or being vulnerable.

I would like to keep 30% of this energy but let go of 70% that is
no longer serving me. I want to take that 30% and further develop it
into ways that maximize my goals and potential. I want to release
myself from any beliefs I might have had about the 70% being
useful or needed. I exhale and release any place my body is holding,
clinging, clenching, or keeping this 70% alive. I am setting it free as
if it no longer serves this version of me.

How does this look for you?

_____

_____

_____

Allow that energy to leave your body. Some examples of how you
can do that are: Let it out on the exhale; release it through conscious
movement, sound, shouts, or yelling, or do an energetic body
brushing.

Then, fill in the space where that old energy lived with positive
energy, unconditional love, and perfect life power. Allow it to ride in

on the inhale or imagine it being delivered to the body in a wave gently washing over you or shining in like a sun beam.

Give yourself permission to receive this. Take a moment to recognize how it feels to have this new life energy move through you.

How does it feel in your body? Which energies do you want to experience more often?

_____

_____

_____

KATHY GATES

Kathy Gates has always been interested in helping people live their best lives.

She is a trained trauma therapist and cross trained in bodywork and somatic release. She is a graduate of Mama Gena's School of Womanly Arts and a licensed Emotional Tour instructor for The Emotional Institute.

She writes from a place of lived experiences, her own and those she has witnessed and guided over the years. She strives to create a pleasure-based life rich with meaning and purpose.

She is the owner and founder of the State College Healing Room, a holistic therapy practice, and the Boldly Feminine Retreat Company, which specializes in creating events and workshops that facilitate women's wellness.

linktr.ee/kjgates

MIRRORS

APRIL LEE

"Knowing yourself is the beginning of all wisdom."
– Confucius

One thing I'm sure of is that your innate power and gifts are unshakable. It's in you, and when you tune in and listen you will find your truth.

From a young age I had strong intuition and knew things about people without them telling me. Sometimes I would feel other people's pain and emotions in my own body, but I lacked the language or understanding to make sense of it. I was drawn to music at an early age, and would play records and sing along for hours on end. I yearned to play a musical instrument and would arrange cups and bowls upside down pretending they were drums and play them with wooden chopsticks.

I was highly sensitive and empathic, and bursting with creative energy. Deep down I knew this was a big part of who I was, but my family didn't allow space for it.

I was raised as an only child in the 70's and 80's by my maternal Chinese-American, Depression-era grandparents. In their pragmatic style, I was housed and clothed, and dinner was on the table every night at the same time, but emotions weren't allowed or discussed. When I tried expressing my creativity, I was shut down.

"I'll get the stick!"

My grandmother would threaten to smack me with a wooden yard stick she used for sewing whenever I stepped out of line. I can still feel the sting of the stick slapping my bare legs. If I cried, she would hit me harder.

I hardly knew my biological parents, having been abandoned by my father when I was only eight months in utero, and my mother when I was five months old. My mother was somewhat present in my life and felt more like an older sister. It was my grandmother who truly embodied the role of a mother. But my father was completely absent from my life. All I knew was that he was a jazz musician who'd struggled with addiction since the time before I was conceived.

I grew up with a sense of mystery and unspoken intensity surrounding my existence in the family. I didn't understand my role or why my grandparents were raising me instead of my parents. I lived in a state of confusion, never truly understanding my life circumstances.

When I was a twenty-year-old college student, I found myself trapped in a cycle of panic attacks. The attacks had become a common occurrence and would sometimes last for hours into the night. They would start off the same way every time: A surge of adrenaline would rush upwards from my belly to my head, and my heart would start racing, filling my entire being with an overwhelming intensity. I would feel disoriented, numb, and terrified. It was like being tossed into the deep sea without a life preserver.

But on one particular evening when I started to feel the familiar sensations of a panic attack coming on, something was different. I was able to pause and witness my experience with awareness. In the space between feeling the first sensations and a full-blown panic attack, I took a moment and observed the situation from the outside looking in. I wondered if there was something I could do to prevent myself from experiencing another night of misery. Then I heard a voice whisper from deep inside my body, "Maybe you're having these panic attacks because you're suppressing your emotions."

As I contemplated the little voice, I felt a sense of deep knowing that screamed, "TRUST IT."

For the first time in my life, I allowed myself to feel. As I opened up, a wave of intense emotions washed over me. I was shaking all over and began to cry.

When I eventually calmed down, I noticed that the panic attack had disappeared. I was in awe. This was the first time I had discovered an innate power to listen to my own inner wisdom and not only feel other peoples' emotions, but my own. I made a vow that I would practice allowing my emotions to come through and give them the space they needed.

As I moved into my 20s, I started exploring the healing arts. I was drawn to the idea of treating the whole person from a body-oriented approach. As I trained in massage therapy and practiced meditation, yoga, and qi gong, I began to feel a sense of connection to myself that I had never experienced before. While doing bodywork, I realized that my intuition and empathic abilities were not only valuable but essential to my work. I began to see my training as a way to not only help others but also to delve more deeply into my own healing process. I was learning about what it meant to get out of my head and connect to my body, listen deeply, and have compassion for myself and for others.

One night when I was in my late 20s, I came home from work to the apartment I shared with my boyfriend, a saxophonist. I walked in the door and my boyfriend said, "There's a message for you on the machine from a guy who sounds like a jazz musician. He said he's your father."

I mustered up the courage to call him back. He said he was on a new path and wanted to connect.

My father drove up from Los Angeles to the San Francisco Bay Area to visit me. As we looked into each other's eyes for the first time on my front porch, it was like looking into a mirror. I saw a reflection of myself in my father, a mix of Japanese and Chinese heritage (a rare occurrence given the historical conflicts between

China and Japan) that I'd never experienced while being raised by my maternal Chinese grandparents. In that moment I felt like I finally understood myself in a way I never had before.

He shared stories from his life filled with music, family, drugs, and trauma. He talked about his addiction, and described his journey to healing and recovery. Part of that journey had involved him becoming a healer. A close Hawaiian friend had passed down his family lineage of Lomi Lomi healing massage to him and he was in the process of developing a private practice.

We had so much in common. My draw to the healing arts and lifelong fascination with music suddenly made so much sense. There was something so familiar about him, something about the way he thought, moved, and talked that resonated with me deeply. It was a feeling I had never experienced before, not even with my biological mother.

That afternoon, my father offered me a Hawaiian Lomi Lomi healing session. I was unfamiliar with this healing tradition and felt a little anxious as he rolled a cream-colored futon mat out onto the floor and asked me to lie on my back. As he smoothed out creases in the futon, I noticed that his arms were covered in tattoos that seemed to tell a million stories that I missed growing up without him. He prepared for the session by kneeling down and chanting a quiet *pu'le* (Hawaiian prayer). I felt the energy in the room shift and become filled with an electric yet grounded potency.

He began by rocking parts of my body back and forth in a fluid and gentle motion, and it felt as if he was creating the space my muscles and joints needed to relax and heal. Simultaneously, I could feel a shift in the energy flowing throughout my body. As the waves of new sensations moved through me, I noticed my curiosity piquing. When I asked what he was doing and why, he laughed and said, "Best to get out of your head and just have the experience." His tone had been non-judgmental yet I could hear myself questioning why I felt such a strong need to know. "Try to let go," I heard him say. So I let my mind be quiet and fell into a deeper state of relaxation as he moved through the session.

His presence felt so familiar despite having only met him a few hours before, and that allowed me to feel safe and trust the process. I drifted in and out of time. Part of me was conscious of being in the room and having my body rocked, stretched, and compressed. Another part of me drifted into a timeless state of being—the eternal moment. I became aware of places in my body where I was holding tension or emotions, and I noticed that he would address these areas and release them. I could sense how meaningful it was for him to share this gift with me. As I received this powerful transmission, it was as if his absence from my life had given way to a reconciliation of my ancestral lineage.

All through the night, I dreamt of Hawaiian spirits chanting and playing drums on a beach. It was as if I was being initiated into a powerful healing tradition through an ancient ritual. The next day, the whiplash injury I'd been struggling with from a car accident was completely healed. I felt an immense sense of relief, as if my body had released all of its tension and my mind had reached a high level of clarity. I had never experienced a healing session like that before and have not since. I sat with the realization that my father was a powerful spiritual healer, a shaman, and I wondered how much pain he'd faced on the journey to embody his true self.

"When the student is ready, the teacher will appear."
- Tao Te Ching

After that first meeting, he and I talked on the phone frequently and made an effort to see each other several times a year. He became my mentor.

One weekend, he passed down his Lomi Lomi to me, as it is traditionally done. I felt that he was handing down not only a physical and spiritual modality, but the source of my essence that helped complete a part of my story that had been missing. I could now be certain that my intuitive power was who I truly was, and that no one could take it away from me.

That was two years into his cancer diagnosis. When he died a year later, it had been fifteen years since we'd first met and stared into each other's eyes. I honored his life and said goodbye from a canoe on Hilo Bay during a traditional Hawaiian ceremony. I celebrated the joy that he and I had experienced through our connection, and knew without a doubt that there was no such thing as lost time.

Through meeting my father, I discovered that the sensitive, intuitive, and empathic being I had always been was a superpower. He helped me see the gift I already had inside of me by reflecting it back and helping me access it.

Now, my intuition and creativity are free to flourish.

WORKSHEET: ANOTHER STEP ON YOUR SPIRAL PATH

OFFERED BY APRIL LEE

Aloha!

It's easy to get caught up in the noise of our minds and distractions around us which can make it difficult to hear our intuition and inner voice. I've created an exercise that will help you quiet your mind, connect with your intuition, and gain clarity. By tapping into the inner wisdom of your heart, you can access your unshakable power.

In Hawaiian culture, aloha is an expression of love, compassion, and kindness.

Alo means presence. *Ha* means breath.

This translates to "Breath of Life."

Aloha can be found at the center of our hearts.

I invite you to tap into the spirit of aloha deep within your own heart.

Create some space

- Find a quiet, comfortable place where you can sit undisturbed.

- Close your eyes for a few gentle breaths, in through your nose and out through your mouth.

Get grounded

- Feel the point of contact between your hips and the surface beneath you. If you're sitting in a chair, feel your feet on the floor.

Relax

- Take a moment and notice if you're feeling any tension.
- Check in with your jaw, shoulders, belly, pelvis, arms, and legs. Relax.

Tune into your awareness

- Notice how it feels to be in your environment, and what's on your mind.
- Bring your attention back to your breath. Let your thoughts go, or let them be present and notice them. If you find your mind wandering off, bring your awareness back to your breath.

Connect to your heart

- Now bring your awareness to your heart and visualize a bright, warm light at the center of your chest. This light can represent your inner voice and intuition.
- When you feel ready, ask your heart a question that has been on your mind. It could be something like, "What do I need to feel more fulfilled in my life?" or "What is the next step on my path?"
- Listen for an answer. It may come as a feeling, a word, an image, a sound, or a sensation.

- Try to let go of judgment or second-guessing what you received. Simply allow it to come through.

Complete

- Come back to the awareness of your breath, to the environment you're sitting in, and open your eyes.

Journal

- You may like to write about your experience and anything that came through.

_____

_____

_____

The more you can relax your body and quiet your mind, the easier it will be to hear your inner voice. If you didn't receive anything, be gentle with yourself and try again another time. With practice it will become easier.

APRIL LEE

April Lee is an intuitive coach, healer, teacher, writer, and mother living in the San Francisco Bay Area. Her life and work are informed by her multicultural upbringing in Berkeley, California, Chinese-Japanese-Irish heritage, and years of personal healing work.

April helps highly sensitive, empathic people learn to listen to their bodies and trust their intuition so they can access their unshakable power and thrive.

She brings decades of experience in Craniosacral therapy, bodywork, embodiment, somatics, mindfulness, meditation, and movement to her coaching practice and group offerings.

April feels most at home when expressing her intuition and creativity, connecting with people, walking among trees and water, exploring the inner and the outer, and living a life of simplicity.

linktr.ee/aprilmlee

SEARCHING FOR THE AMERICAN DREAM

SUSAN K. SMITH

I 'm sitting in a Dubai theater watching *Nomadland*, a 2020 film depicting the demise of the small town of Empire, Nevada, and its residents' financial devastation. The film's primary character is an older female, played by Frances McDormand, who joins an army of others who can't pay their mortgages, live in vans, and migrate from job to job. Thankfully, the nomads are depicted with dignity and respect as they openly applaud themselves for their houseless status and celebrate the open-road adventure.

I become increasingly angry and agitated in the theater's darkness.

"Is this the American dream, being forced to choose between the comforts of home or living in a van?"

Still, though, I do empathize with their plight. I could have been one of those houseless nomads if I hadn't driven through a red light one day in 2004.

It was a typical, muggy Oklahoma summer day, with the mercury exceeding a hundred degrees Fahrenheit and heat waves bouncing off the pavement. Driving down Tulsa's Yale Avenue, there are two traffic lights, one right after the other, a block apart. The first light was green, but I went through the second, a red light, without stopping. To my horror, I drove smack into the driver's side of a police vehicle, wrecking it but hurting no one.

What I remember most about hitting the police car was not the utter shock and stupidity of the crash. Or the annoying man, adrenaline pumping, yelling at me about how fast I was going. Or the local news crews who arrived at the scene to spread images of the wreck. What I told the policeman when he asked me what had happened is forged in my mind. Aware of the utter ridiculousness of my situation, I muttered, looking him squarely in the eyes without hesitating, "I am upset about the U.S. war in Iraq." The policeman walked away, noting my name in his little pad and not raising an eyebrow or questioning my response.

The crash pushed me to my limits. My poverty was stifling. I felt ashamed because I couldn't lift myself by my bootstraps, the American way of advancement. The 9/11 climate of "hate" toward the Middle East further ignited my anger, and within me brewed a furious contempt for U.S. policies.

I was stuck.

I don't belong here!

How had I gotten to this point?

What was wrong with me?

I needed a different view.

When I was two, I climbed a colossal oak tree in our yard and couldn't get down. As the firefighters rescued me, I squinted into the horizon of limitless possibilities and thought, "Someday, I will go to the far edges of the world!"

At fifty-two years old, I stepped towards freedom.

The American dream my parents achieved was as far out of reach for me now as twenty-five years earlier when I started my university journey. While my white privilege helped–I worked with wealthy clients for whom I did manual labor to earn a man's wage, and my graduate degree was acquired at a private university–I faced the challenges of being female, a single parent, and working day and night to gain financial prosperity in a capitalistic system that propagated income inequality.

I suffered from depression throughout those years of hardship. I paid for sliding-scale therapy to combat feelings of inadequacy. Time and time again, I was told that it was my perception and low self-esteem which hampered my success; all the while, the therapist ignored the system that throttled me.

That system pressed me between forces. As a woman, every decision produced devastating consequences, causing me to re-examine without mercy my broken relationships and my introversion (which I hear is a new sensitivity these days).

All these so-called failures created negative self-talk:

Why couldn't I do better?

I'm too shy and not friendly enough.

I'm just not working hard enough!

Self-blame and deep shame took root, crushing my self-image even more.

After graduate school, with the expectation of turning my life around, my financial situation did not improve.

I was vulnerable, and twenty-five years of persistent poverty traumatized me.

Hard work, graduate education, resilience, and stubbornness produced the same outcome: I had not reached that American Dream.

Harboring a disillusioned heart, I applied for an overseas professor position in the Middle Eastern country of the United Arab Emirates (UAE) in 2004. While I was highly qualified for the job, my university connections and luck cemented the deal. Yet, I had reservations about leaving my family and friends.

Many emotions quivered through me like an electrical shock.

"This is what I need to do," I told myself.

Still, I asked myself:

We are constantly told that the "grass isn't greener on the other side."

Am I looking for answers in the wrong place?

What if I leave the United States and don't find greener pastures in the Islamic Kingdom of the UAE?

I would be alone in a Muslim country, raising a young child in my fifties and starting a new academic career there.

My relatives warned me that I would get my hand cut off if I wasn't careful.

Was I being impulsive?

Was I heading for danger?

This time, I went full speed ahead, and *not* into the door of a police car!

I left America and everyone I loved.

As a newly appointed custodial grandparent of Ivy, aged eight, we ventured, hand-in-hand, with bags packed, to the UAE. Despite the warnings, I felt the "rightness of my decision" in my bones. I taught documentary film at the American University of Sharjah.

With this move, I could afford excellent healthcare and feed Ivy and myself without choosing between keeping warm and paying rent or school loans. For the first time, I would live the life I imagined possible.

I hadn't planned to live abroad for eighteen years.

Still, life unfolded, bringing personal losses, rewards, and professional ups and downs. I continued to make documentaries that took me to faraway places throughout the Middle East, Africa, and Asia, rewarding me with many rich friendships.

Over time, I also created a wonderful and diverse family abroad.

I developed one of my most cherished friendships with Nancy, a Maasai woman who grew up with five moms living in the foothills of Mount Kilimanjaro, Kenya.

Nancy's life and mine intersected in 2003, before my move to UAE, when I journeyed to Kima, Kenya, Nancy's hometown, to shoot a documentary about educating the Maasai girl-child. The documentary centered around a fateful day decades ago when, at age thirteen, Nancy learned she was to be married to a man three times her age and how, in unheard-of defiance, Nancy revolted against her family's wishes. Nancy spoke up for her right to continue her education, choose when and whom to marry, and pursue the dream of living the life she wanted. As a result, she was chased away from her family.

With few options before her and for reasons I can understand, Nancy left her village and moved to Loitokitok, a smaller nearby Kenyan town.

Throughout our friendship, our lives moved in parallel directions.

Sitting on my back porch in UAE in 2019, with tiny birds flitting and feeding on my Captain Cook bottle brush blooms, Nancy wrote the story of her life while I, too, worked on my memoir.

Our experiences are as different as they are similar, as individual as they are universal.

We talked about how she escaped an early marriage and how her wedding refusal inspired many other young girls in her village. It slowed the girls' pace of getting matched while in school and made it easier for them to excel at university and marry the man they chose.

Nancy listened as I shared, "I was married at eighteen." I recounted my limited options as a young woman growing up in the Midwest in the 60s and 70s.

Ironically, but not surprisingly, we shared some of the same obstacles. For example, our families were willing to educate our brothers but not help with our education.

Education is a core element in establishing freedom and economic independence.

As young women, we were both denied this freedom.

Our conversation shifted to the non-profit organizations we each created. Nancy's organization is NAWODEN, a network of women designed to support young girls staying in school and escaping arranged marriages. Inspired by Nancy, my non-profit, Speak Trauma Foundation, gives agency to many women who speak up. The foundation gave me a further sense of purpose while living abroad and provided a spiritual connection to others.

There is a saying in Arabic culture, taken from the context of the Quran, that roughly translates to silence as a sign of consent.

While some dispute this interpretation, most agree that staying silent is a self-preservation method. Keeping women quiet is culturally implemented by attaching labels—recalcitrant or unruly, disobedient, noncompliant, stubborn, and obstinate—to control women's speech and behavior.

The UAE culture practices "benign feminism." In this culture, social and legal implications are linked solely to women's behavior and cultural expectations (*Bootstrapped: Liberating Ourselves from the American Dream* by Alissa Quart, 2022).

With recent Harvey Weinstein convictions and the worldwide MeToo movement, our Western cultures still cultivate young girls to be pleasant and agreeable. And, for many young girls worldwide, their only weapon is obedience, something Nancy turned her back on.

Sometimes I wonder if my situation would have been different if I had, like Nancy, spoken up and told my parents that I deserve and want an education, that I want to live to my fullest potential!

With that possibility now long gone, Speak Trauma Foundation is a bridge to allowing others to live their full potential. It empowers women to speak up and share their experiences by providing agency and creating a storytelling platform for women. In many ways, the organization offers women the healing and validation to feel less alone as they scan their horizons for limitless possibilities.

Speak Trauma teaches documentary skills to the participants and offers a safe place for them to share their stories without shame and judgment.

For instance, we have held space for Mijikenda women in Mombasa who have lost their loved ones to recruitment by Al

Shabab (a terrorist organization) and Zanzibari youths who strive to improve their filmmaking skills so they, too, can capture the rich stories of their fellow Zanzibaris.

In retrospect, my gut reaction to the film *Nomadland* was fitting in that it brings the view of my life into more explicit focus.

The film is based on Jessica Bruder's 2017 non-fiction book, *Nomadland: Surviving America in the Twenty-First Century*. The book more aptly describes the poverty and social issues experienced by many American women, with only an occasional glorification of the houseless experience.

Did I find the American dream while residing in the peaceful Islamic kingdom of the UAE?

As with every country, many injustices must be acknowledged when measuring equality. During my eighteen years in the UAE, I have witnessed enormous changes in the government and citizens' viewpoints and understanding of others. The UAE still has a long way to go to be more inclusive, but the younger, educated residents, some of whom I taught, are shaping new opportunities for themselves and less fortunate others. I am not an authority on living in the UAE, but my nearly two decades there have given me a bigger picture of life abroad.

With my professor's tenure ending, I am stepping into something that looks like retirement, and I have chosen to return to the United States.

Returning to America at seventy years old, I am constantly reminded of my vulnerability. I am bombarded with articles about how to save more money, reports about medical bills that can cause bankruptcy, how to avoid Alzheimer, and my growing dependency on the American Medicare system as I age. Added to this is "hostile" feminism that continues to flourish in the United States (*Bootstrapped: Liberating Ourselves from the American Dream* by Alissa Quart, 2022).

Growing old and being a single female in America is something to reckon with.

When I left America nearly twenty years ago, I understood the American Dream was a myth. I also knew I didn't belong, and looking for that place to call home sent me on my journey living abroad.

It is time for a new American Dream. Envisioning my future, my Speak Trauma Foundation, and my documentary filmmaking, I am drawn toward providing agency through storytelling for older adults. I want to raise awareness about income inequality and confront the system that has created millions of vulnerable people in America.

Upon returning to America, my homeland, thankfully I won't have to sell my house, live in a van, and become houseless (keeping my fingers crossed about this last point, for in America, nothing is guaranteed).

I achieved a version of the American Dream while living abroad that now gives me enough economic independence to live the life I choose…and I'm choosing to return as a more empowered version of myself.

Even while I will be far away from my family abroad, a family I have come to love, I know they won't be far from my heart.

I vow to create another family back in my homeland of America.

In some absolute sense, I am, and forever will be, a nomad, always reaching for limitless possibilities on those distant horizons.

WORKSHEET: ANOTHER STEP ON YOUR SPIRAL PATH

OFFERED BY SUSAN K. SMITH

The fallacy of the American Dream is that hard work is needed to make it in America. But in reality, the American system rewards the wealthy (primarily, rich from inheritance and not hard work) and spins a lie, starting with the belief that we have equal opportunities.

I was ahead of my time when I chose to move abroad, and being aware that the American Dream was a myth, changed my journey. Today, numerous books are challenging the American Dream. I highly recommend reading *Bootstrapped: Liberating Ourselves from the American Dream* by Alissa Quart (2022).

Government Programs:

Before deciding to move abroad for employment, consider seeking government assistance. Consider it as taking part in a system of "interdependence."

Spiritual Purpose:

Living with purpose is essential to finding fulfillment, and if we are going to work, it is a good idea to "spin" our energy on creating meaning in our lives.

Education:

Grab new learning opportunities to help you get a new position or improve your chances. The government will loan most women, particularly single women with children, large amounts. I stress here, loan, not give. And these loans will grow with interest throughout the years. Invest in it if this is the only way to get an education.

Foreign Resident Status:

You will be a foreign resident (with fewer civil rights). This can mean that if any law is broken, consequences might affect your residency status, just as we see for non-citizens living in the United States. Most of us are law-abiding citizens, but negotiating a foreign legal system can be intimidating.

Benefits: Federal and State taxes

As a resident of a foreign country (depending on the length of stay), you will not be required to pay federal income taxes above a pre-specified income level. You will have to pay state property taxes if you own U.S. property. You will be required to do annual tax returns. Not paying taxes boosts your yearly income while living and working abroad.

Employment:

Work for a company that supplies you with a rent-free accommodation or a compensation package that provides substantial benefits. My company offered a residence visa and an excellent indemnity package, making it easier to navigate living abroad.

SUSAN K. SMITH

Susan K. Smith is a documentary filmmaker and professor (Visual Anthropologist) living abroad in the United Arab Emirates (UAE) for eighteen years.

Her ex-pat identity developed from a deep need to understand herself and American culture. Susan's life abroad also required her to make a conscious effort to understand other cultures. In doing so, this awareness demands that she constantly re-examine her cultural beliefs.

Susan's documentary-making has transitioned from telling other people's stories to teaching cinematic storytelling skills to others, motivating them to speak their truth.

linktr.ee/speaktraumafoundation

CRONE LEARNING TO DANCE WITH DEATH

ELLISON JAMES

I stood at the front of the classroom at the unemployment office, taking it all in. Hearing the clapping. Seeing the huge smiles on people's faces. Noticing the teacher's mouth still gaping in surprise.

"Pay attention to this!" a little whisper urged. "Nobody gets a standing ovation at unemployment."

Little did I know at that moment what had just taken place or how it might change my life.

After all, my life was pretty good, wasn't it? I had a safe roof over my head, a good car to drive, and meaningful work that I enjoyed and was well suited for.

I had never really bought into the popular notion that being a success meant being rich and famous.

It was okay that I hadn't followed the path I had expected. I never turned into a 1950's sitcom housewife like I had grown up watching on TV every night during dinner. There was no standing at the stove in my ruffled apron, waiting for my husband to come home so I could greet him at the door with a kiss, then serve him the dinner I had lovingly prepared.

What there was, were many years as a single mom, working hard at manual labor jobs and eating take-out or drive-through.

After my son was grown and gone, life had become easier, allowing me to take a deep breath and see what was next.

I was loved by my clients and co-workers. I was excellent at my job as a private hospice and Alzheimer's caregiver. To me, this was success. That, in the past year, I had made more money than I ever had, was just a cherry on top.

When my more than full-time hospice client died, I was left unemployed. So here I was once again, standing at one of life's many crossroads. We all get to learn to navigate these twists and turns. It's just easier if you are paying attention. And I was paying attention.

With 20 years experience escorting frail, white-haired elders across the threshold of life, I was not afraid to be unemployed. I felt grateful to be here at an unemployment class learning how to best present my qualifications to a potential new employer and wondering what my next adventure would be.

Now it was my turn to come to the podium. Standing with my head held high, and my voice clear, I comfortably rattled off my many qualifications: 4.0 grades in school; advanced Alzheimer's training, and a medical assistant certification. A few minutes ago, these had seemed so important. Yet, now, as we practiced this week's lesson, mastering the elevator speech, I acknowledged how little significance should be given to what I had just said.

I assured the class that there was a better reason to hire me. And for the first time, I believed it.

Suddenly my heart began to race and my throat felt tight and dry. I looked around the stark, cold, beige room, hearing the fluorescent lights flickering, thirty pairs of expectant eyes on me. None of us had any idea of what was going to come out of my mouth.

Then, I felt myself expanding to fill the room, telling myself I was safe and it was time to follow the divine inspiration I was about to receive. It was as if I was floating slightly above myself, just watching everything unfold.

I stood up a little straighter, looked directly at the teacher and blurted out this outrageous claim.

"The reason I should be hired is because of my superpower."

I paused for dramatic effect and watched as everyone leaned in, not wanting to miss what was coming.

"My ability to hold the enormity of grief and fear during a loved one's dying is what makes me a death doula. My superpower is death!"

The ensuing standing ovation startled me a little, but when the teacher called for a break, and a dozen fellow students came to me excitedly sharing their own stories of loved ones dying, it confirmed which direction I would take at this crossroad. I heard over and over again, "This is so important! Nobody talks about death," and, "I wish I had someone there for me when my family member or dear friend was dying."

I would like to tell you how this turning point instantly changed my life, but that's not how it worked.

For most, life is not a clear straight path from beginning to end. For me, it wasn't even a matter of a few course corrections. Mine has been a series of invitations to run directly into the fire...I mean, growth opportunities...then, for a while, live in the pause of practicing.

I didn't realize in that moment of claiming my gift that I was being thrown into a preparatory pot to marinade. I needed the next seven years to grow into my next iteration of self.

What an interesting path I was on.

Now the question was: *What path am I on?*

Maybe a more important question would be: *How the hell did I get here?*

Since I knew my life path wasn't a straight line, I needed to see if somehow the past would give me a clue to the next steps into my future.

I grew up in the San Francisco Bay Area during the 60s, a time of the hippies and the Black Panthers and burning our bras. I love that I'm part of a generation that strongly questioned authority and believed in love not war (not that our marches changed how our government has acted, but that's a different story). We strove to march to our own drum beat, and not just follow the rules, but reinvent them.

So it's interesting how easily my midwestern parents sold me on their version of the American dream. You know, the rigid plan that promised that if I went to school, got good grades, I could get into a good college. That was how I could get a good job, work hard, and make a lot of money and, hopefully, someday find someone to love and take care of me, which honestly felt a little bit like rescuing me...blah...blah...blah...have kids, pay bills, scrimp and save so someday I could retire with a gold watch and then do what I wanted.

As a self-proclaimed non-conformist, seeing how much fitting in played in the background and influenced too many of my choices, makes my stomach do a couple of flip flops like the whirly ride at the amusement park.

I made the best choices I could with what I knew when navigating opportunities placed before me. No college, no prince charming to rescue me (thank goodness).

As I age, I could complain or cry. Let the loss of parents, friends, youth, or time invite me to give up as many seniors do. I don't.

Our upbringing certainly colors the lens through which we see life, but I have to acknowledge the strong impact our experience also has on the choices we make, ultimately molding the person we become and the life we end up with.

All these years of claiming death as my superpower have proved to be a fertile ground where I could grow into myself, and let go of the constant searching and grabbing for validation from others. When I stopped looking outside of myself to feel like I was good enough, and started finding the answers inside myself, life got a lot sweeter.

Don't get me wrong, there were plenty of years I was sucked into the harmful claims put out by corporations that if I just bought their designer shoes, clothes, cars, and everything else they were selling, that I would be happy. Or the brainwashing that if I was just thin enough or blonde enough with long legs and big breasts, then I would be good enough.

Now I laugh at how ridiculous it looks to think the path to enough was through more. To buy more, work more, diet more. Just try harder. It turns out that the only thing that guarantees is burnout, with stress levels through the roof and energy levels in the basement. Thank goodness that was just a temporary detour.

I spent those marinating seven years wisely, following the archetype of Priestess. I connected the mundane aspects of caregiving with the sacred ritual of dying. I hold that we are born into this life and we are born out of this life—both equally sacred and precious. Any of you that have held someone's hand as they take their last breath will understand.

My time as a death doula provided me with numerous opportunities to learn to dance with death. I will always be grateful for the moments when I could reassure a client in their last hours by telling them that they were surrounded by loved ones who would miss them enormously, but that it would be alright. Then offer permission to go ahead and go whenever they wanted to. I am also thankful for the moments of grace…like the time I was inspired to grab the bedside lip balm, spread it on my client's dry lips and tell her that she needed to have nice moist lips to smooch her husband when he greeted her in heaven; a sly little smile crossed her now-moist lips.

As a death doula, I've also held space for the families. Part of what makes it hard is when everyone is trying to be brave and stoic so as not to upset anyone else. It's important for me to provide them with the time and opportunity to wail their fear and grief in my safe presence.

One of my most memorable clients had a daughter on the team of caregivers. I usually came on shift to relieve her. As her mother entered the active phase of dying, which can take anywhere from twenty-four hours to several days, I could see how resistant this daughter was to letting go. Both the hospice nurse and I had told her several times that it's okay to let her mom not eat. The fierce mother in this daughter must have believed that if she could just get her mom enough nutrients, she could save her. I came on shift that last day only to find her trying to force her mom to eat. I could feel the franticness in this loving daughter. So I reached up to gently move the spoon full of pudding and her hand away. When I explained to her that her mother was never going to eat or drink again, that it was painful for her mother, she recoiled as if I had thrown cold water in her face. That grief-stricken look on her face broke my heart, as much as her tears showed me that her heart was broken, too.

What I know from these precious years is that some people prefer to die alone and will wait for you to leave. Other people prefer to be surrounded by loved ones and will wait for you to come. Since we have no way of knowing, I always recommend alternating between being present and being absent, and letting death take its own course.

Death's course comes with lessons for all of us. I learned one of them from a client's grandson.

While we were all having dinner, a client passed. Her grandson was so devastated that I suggested that we take his dog for a walk. Once outside, he sobbed, grabbing my hand and saying that I had been an island of peace for him at the hardest time of his life. That testimonial made all those years worthwhile…and prepared me to start celebrating the crone I had become.

Crone is really about learning to dance with life and death.

Through all the experiences of life, its greatest joys and its greatest sorrows, we learn to build our capacity to hold the intensity of our feelings. In this, we become a giant container to hold incredible space for others, especially those we love. This is the root of our wisdom. And it's hard earned.

I write this to invite you to look at aging and death through a different lens than is traditional in modern culture. We are not less desirable or valuable as we age. The dictionary defines crone as a withered old ugly woman. I call bullshit on that.

The word crone comes from crown. And I say yes, we are old women wearing the crown of wisdom. We are sovereign.

Ladies, we are all on the same path!

Welcome to The Path to Crone. Like it or not, you bought the ticket just by being born.

And the only way off is death.

In the meantime, let's step out of our marinade, put on our crowns, and dance with life.

WORKSHEET: ANOTHER STEP ON YOUR SPIRAL PATH

OFFERED BY ELLISON JAMES

Curiosity has always served me well. I invite you to bring that to this page of prompts.

You can play with this any way you want:

Curled up before a fire with a cup of tea, your journal and a favorite pen. Sitting at a beach, deep in conversation, toes wiggling in the damp sand, inspired by a sunset. In your studio, paint brush in hand or glue pictures to a collage. Draw, paint, doodle, journal or just some good old pondering.

Visit this over and over again and see how your answers shift.

How old is old? (& why)

_____

_____

_____

When I'm old, I will

_____
_____
_____

When my loved one dies, here's how I'd like to be comforted

_____
_____
_____

How is life nurturing or cultivating my wisdom?

_____
_____
_____

Tackle them all at one time or choose one to focus on and spend plenty of time reflecting on your answers.

HAVE FUN & ENJOY.

ELLISON JAMES

Ellison James is a poet, artist, ceremonialist, and wild idea woman living in the Pacific Northwest.

She works with vibrant ambitious women who want to increase their energy so that they can live their big, bold dream lives.

She follows a divinely inspired life of service with a strong emphasis on seasonal alignment. Through this, she has created a new model of productivity to avoid burnout.

Decades of experience as a private hospice and Alzheimer's caregiver has prepared her to embrace aging and has invited into her new Sovereign Crone work.

linktr.ee/ellisonjames

THE WIND THAT WHISPERS TO ME

JENNIFER BALJKO

I click the heels of my hiking boots three times, hopeful something will happen, that my wish will be fulfilled.

"I want to go home. I want to go home. I. WANT. TO. GO. HOME." I yell for dramatic effect, choking on the tears I'd rather cry, but don't because that would be a wasteful use of salt and water. My voice wanders over the blacktop stretching out forever and going nowhere in particular.

I'm not Dorothy. I'm not in Oz. And I don't have ruby red shoes.

I'm Jenn. Walking Jenn. No good witch is coming to save me from my own choice to be here.

Here…is the middle of Uzbekistan. In July. The sun scorches this Central Asian country with its 45+ Celsius (113+ Fahrenheit) temperature. The soles of my shoes make a gooey schloooop sound with each arduous step, and it takes extra effort to lift my feet from the melting asphalt. Wrapped head to toe to protect every part of my flesh from the killing afternoon sun, I tuck my face scarf under the edges of my glasses to stop the hot air from drying out my eyes.

Home…Barcelona…is thousands of kilometers away from where

I am, and the way I will get there is by walking three kilometers an hour, for years.

This lonely road is one of the many paths connecting my heart's biggest desire to be wildly free and the footsteps it takes to achieve that. Bangkok Barcelona On Foot is the magic my love and life partner Lluís and I chose to make in the decade called our 40s. As the name implies, we intend to—and we will—walk the 16,000-kilometer (almost 10,000-mile) distance between those two cities. The subtitle of our walk is "Exploring the world, seeking the goodness of people," and what we find will influence our lives ever after.

The idea took seed three years earlier when a wind whispered to me, summoning me to this particular adventure, and I, once again, decided to listen.

Every once in a while, a wind that's mine to hear rises up, and every time it does, it causes a pivot, forces an unexpected and courageous shift of direction, and rattles my confidence. The last time it happened, a string of words floated in on a warm June Mediterranean wind and offered this instruction, "Before you're old and broken, go for a long, long walk."

Surprisingly, Lluís, my wanderlust-loving soulmate, also wanted to follow this cosmic breadcrumb. Together we gave life an enthusiastic YES! and began the work of saving for, planning, and being comfortable with the disruption a multi-year trek would ignite. Without fully understanding what we committed to and feigning fearlessness in the face of the million small and big things that could possibly go wrong at any twist and turn, we leapt in, guessing a net would appear in ways we couldn't yet fathom.

Along the length of the walk, a nagging thought would often creep through my mind's dark corners: If this is what Spirit had in mind for my higher self's purpose, the joke must be on me.

I constantly ask myself, "Really, who **WALKS** two continents... not one... **TWO** continents? Who does this kind of thing?"

Apparently, we do, and I will wonder about the "Why?" underscoring this journey for years to come, sometimes relishing the choice we made to do this very hard thing and other times kicking myself for taking on the most difficult physical, emotional, and mental challenge I have ever endured.

Uzbekistan proves to be just another test in a long battery of tests that try to break me and gets ever closer to succeeding.

Lluís walks ahead of me. He's always ahead of me. For the 10 years we've been together as a couple, we have walked different paces. His is an urban gait, that of a man on a mission with a destination in clear view. Mine is that of a woman going the scenic route and taking time to look around and smell the roses.

Carrying 20-odd kilograms—about 45 pounds—on my back (including six liters of water) makes me even slower. Truly, it's an unbearable stride. I can only keep learning how to bear it. It's either that or quit. I've tried to quit, too many times, like 100 times a day, but I can't. I won't. There's something to accomplish, something more important than me hidden in the map of life I'm not yet privy to see. Somehow, the universe trusts that I'm the person to navigate this path. So, the only way forward is through.

Lluís waits for me at the row of barricades randomly placed in the middle of the parched moonscape, marking the shoulder of the road. He points to the sliver of shade behind the blocks, the only shade we've seen for miles.

"Be careful. There's a spider," he says as I throw my backpack on the ground.

I glance to my right and see the yellow-bodied being hanging upside down in the center of its web. With its legs stretched out, it is as big as my hand. A couple years ago, this creature would have scared the bejesus out of me. Today, I barely lift my eyebrows, too exhausted to give away my energy. I nod to the spider, admiring the intricate beauty of her web, and ask her if we can share her space. I hope her silence is consent or a sign of her curiosity.

"It's so, so hard today. It's so hot. I'm so thirsty." I say, leaning back on the concrete, reaching for my water bottle. The water is not at all refreshing, but it is critical. "Remind me: Why are we doing this? Who's idea was this?"

Lluís chuckles as he reaches out for my hand.

We both know how this foot journey—which we started on my

forty-fourth birthday and would complete in three and a half years—unfolded.

It was that irresistible and irrefutable whisper that was mine to hear… and ours to act on.

The first time I remember hearing this kind of whisper, said with the clarity and authority of a being beyond me, I was five years old.

One fall day, something like "Pack up and go. It's time," came from somewhere, caught my attention, and landed in my heart.

"Ok," I must have said as I packed underwear, socks, and t-shirts into my bubblegum pink Barbie doll suitcase.

Ready to go, I walked into the kitchen and said goodbye to my mother. "I'm off to see the world," I extolled.

She glanced over, still stirring the sweet corn niblets coming to a boil. She squinted her eyes with suspicion, but remained undaunted. Maybe she knew way back then that I would be her odd child, the one always so willing to leave. "Dinner will be ready in fifteen minutes," she said, dishing out her Mom tone. I felt her eyes following towards the front door.

I waved to my dad. He waved back. He was watching a football game, so the only question on his mind was, "Did they get the first down?" A good omen for me, to be sure. Any other questions would have had me fumbling over the feelings I couldn't express.

All I knew was that life had invited me to say YES!, and I did.

I was brave. I was bold. I was most definitely keen to try.

Then I was crushed.

I got as far as the corner when that niggling matter surfaced, the one that frequently comes after taking the first steps on an unmarked trail: Now what?

I wasn't allowed to cross the street and I wasn't old enough to turn the corner by myself without an adult. I was allowed, sort of, kind of, to go to the STOP sign, the boundary of my five-year-old liberty.

I did as I was told. I stopped.

I puzzled over what to do next.

Should I break the rules and keep going?

What happens if I get caught breaking the rules?

How could I NOT break the rules if I really wanted to explore the world the way I wanted to?

Who made these rules anyway?

If I broke the rules and I kept going, would I go up to the heavily trafficked boulevard and dare myself to cross the street? Or do I go down the hill, towards the creepy broken staircase littered by weeds and who knows what grossness?

And… if I did all that…then what?

Important choices had to be made. Everything I wanted—freedom, adventure, independence—seemed to be dangling right in front of me.

Then I got scared.

How would I take care of myself?

What if I got hurt?

Where would I sleep?

How would I know if I'm going the right way?

Then I got hungry.

It was the rumble in my tummy that turned the choice-making options into a practical decision: Life can wait. The world will still be there. Go home and eat.

During a walk across two continents, in the getting from there to here to way over there, there are many empty miles to ponder life's mysteries. Uzbekistan is filled with them, these long stretches of gently rolling, boring nothingness.

In these moments, I mull over the accumulation of my choices and outcomes, judging them, assessing what I learned from them. Often, I revisit the significant milestone moments that the wind guided me to chase.

"Remember when you heard 'You don't have to live in New Jersey your whole life. Go west,' and you moved to San Francisco! That was a good choice," I smile with pride, seeing the 25-year-old version of myself driving my red Toyota Tercel through Golden Gate Park.

"Then there was that *Eat, Pray, Love* moment, and that cute naked guy at the beach." I flinch. In a nanosecond of heartbroken sadness on the edge of signing divorce papers, a meaningful conversation with a stranger, quite literally showing me his everything, gave me hope. An hour later, driving on Interstate 280, right under the Daly City signpost, I heard, "Save all your money. Quit your job in six months. Backpack through Europe."

That choice led me a few months later to Lluís, who I met in the middle of a Barcelona plaza packed with thousands of festival-goers. The same Lluís I barely see in front of me now.

To outsmart the utterly exhausting heat, we've begun walking at night. The strategy doesn't work as well as we thought it would. Our rest breaks and sleep patterns are completely messed up. In all ways, we're always tired.

For whatever reason, Lluís turns off his flashlight. Seeing only the outline of his backpack a few meters in front of me, I concentrate on the shadow of his shape.

Even with my headlamp shining bright enough, I'm too drowsy to notice my footfall. I fall asleep walking, and tip sideways, hitting the ground with a thump so hard my glasses fly off my face. Lluís circles back to help me up.

"Wait. Don't step on my glasses," I cry, this time not holding back the tears and gulping in the pain, frustration, discouragement, embarrassment. I have to unstrap my pack and crawl onto all fours so I can stand again. The sting of salt burns my eyes, and the scrape on my right hand hurts less than my anger.

Lluís lifts my backpack off the ground and helps me sling it back on my shoulders…a weight I keep choosing to carry because of some voice… some part of me… that believes this is a piece of my life's puzzle.

Regaining my humped-over stride, I bust out laughing at the absurdity of it all. Not just at the bizarre goal called Bangkok Barcelona On Foot, but at my naive willingness to do this strange, unconventional thing.

"What's wrong with me...with us? Why do we have to do this? What are we trying to prove?" I sigh and wait for the answer.

A soft breeze catches the night, and a tiny, quiet voice passes through me.

"Look up."

I tilt my head back, and the tears slowly come again. This time they are the tears of wonder, awe, and joy.

I stand absolutely still, thumbs hooked around my backpack straps. The sky is lit with more stars than I have ever seen in my entire life. The creamy band of the Milky Way holds my breath.

When I remember to exhale, the voice returns. "Do you see it now?"

I wait for my own answer.

"Yes, I do." I say out loud with renewed confidence.

A flash of memory connects me to my five-year-old self at the STOP sign, the little girl who knew life called to her.

"I'm so willing to be here and do this absurd thing because... I am part of all of this. I'm part of the beautiful intricate web life is always weaving."

"Yes, and..." I hear as another almost unperceivable breeze caresses my cheeks.

I pause and ponder. And, then I know.

The knowing fills my body, and I stand up a little taller.

"Oh....I am a weaver."

Knowing the profound human experience of being part of creating all there is, all there was, and all that will be, keeps my eyes fixed on the sky.

I take a long, slow inhale. I want to linger. I want to cherish everything about this fleeting moment.

But there's still work to do. There's more life to live.

I nod, once again saying YES! to whatever comes next. I exhale with sigh, sending my consent back out into the world on the back of a breeze.

I turn off my headlamp and step forward into a darkness lit by a million stars.

WORKSHEET: ANOTHER STEP ON
YOUR SPIRAL PATH

OFFERED BY JENNIFER BALJKO

Take a moment to come back to this present moment, using your breath as a guide to connect your belly, heart, and mind—the centers of your intuition, emotional well-being, and intellect.

Allow yourself to remember a moment in your life that required courage to change directions. Feel, sense, know, see, or hear how that moment unfolded.

Write a few sentences about one of your important pivots, AHA! moments, or fierce awakenings.

_____

_____

_____

What else was happening at the time? Zoom in and see the small details. Zoom out and see the big picture.

_____

_____

_____

Where did that fierce awakening take you, in that moment and gradually over time? What other forks in the road, opportunities, and choices showed up after that AHA! moment?

_____

_____

_____

Notice how a variety of choices and outcomes have accumulated over your lifetime. Sometimes, they may have guided you to joy, wonder, awe, and a sense of achievement and happiness. Other times, the path may have detoured you through fear, hurt, sadness, and disappointment. They have all added up to where you are now.

Connect the dots. Weave a short story about how these choices, pivots, and outcomes have added up and have become a part of your own unique profound human experience.

_____

_____

_____

Take a deep breath, and with tenderness, patience, integrity, and grace, ask yourself, "Now what?"

Wait. There's no rush. An answer will rise. Now. Tomorrow. Next month. Give yourself space and time to know. Trust that a wind meant for you to hear and act on will come.

When you're ready, write the answer to "Now what?"

_____

_____

_____

Be willing to weave your next step into life's intricate and beautiful web. Say YES! to life's invitation, Fierce One!

Mind map ideas, inspirations, and memories of past pivots to help shape the path you are inventing now, the path that connects you to all that is and all you're meant to be.

_____

_____

_____

Additional resources: linktr.ee/jennbaljko

JENNIFER BALJKO

FIERCE AWAKENINGS' LEAD AUTHOR AND DEVELOPMENTAL EDITOR

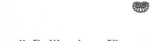

Jennifer "Jenn" Baljko is a Fierce Awakened Woman Way-Maker, helping women step forward with courage, confidence, and creative chutzpah. She nurtures Joy Journeys, and guides people through personal pivots and professional reinvention. Jenn helps women navigate mid-life breakdowns, breakthroughs, and fierce awakenings so they can live with more creativity, joy, and wonder.

In parallel, Jenn mentors aspiring authors and draws on nearly thirty years of journalism, writing, and editing experience as a developmental book editor.

As a certified mindfulness meditation teacher and licensed Emotional Tour instructor for The Emotional Institute, Jenn holds space for the deep emotional release and healing that comes when we lower the volume of our racing thoughts and connect to our body's natural rhythms.

She counts the completion of a 3.5-year walk across two continents, from Bangkok to Barcelona, as one of her most significant achievements.

linktr.ee/jennbaljko

POSTSCRIPT: WHAT'S NEXT FOR YOU?

Congratulations on reaching this rest stop on the spiral path. Take a breath. Celebrate how far you have come now and in life. Choose and cultivate the next steps on your onward journey.

We hope our stories have created an enriching experience for you and inspired an array of *AHA!* revelations.

While we're on the last pages of this book, we are also at another beginning point. As we've cycled through our individual and collective heroine's journeys, we've climbed one rung higher on the spiral with greater insight into our own lived experiences. From this moment's perspective, we ask you the same question we are asking ourselves: What's next?

In many ways, the mindful contemplation, meaningful conversations, and imaginative sparks that come after you put this book down may lead to any number of fresh starts, new opportunities, and surprising next steps.

Based on the collaborative intuition we nurtured with and beyond this book, we see how the power of self-discovery is strengthened through connecting, sharing, and weaving together ideas, possibilities, and wisdom.

From this heart-centered belief, we encourage and invite you to start your own women's circle or book club to explore the deeper knowing that surpasses the words on these pages. Embracing this phase of the adventure will provide a valuable tool for personal growth, reflection, and lifelong learning for yourself and so many others.

If you're willing to be a *Fierce Awakenings* way-maker and help bring women together so they can share more of their unique gifts and tell their stories, we offer these questions as starting points for sincere dialogue.

- What does walking a spiral path mean to you?
- Where are you now on the spiral path? Which experiences would you put in the center of the spiral, and what else evolves and revolves from that center?
- What does belonging feel like to you, and who or what nourishes this sense of belonging?
- Have you guarded your heart, and if so, why?
- How have you honored your pain and grief? How does being with grief illuminate love, wisdom, and belonging?
- Who have you met along the way that changed the course of your life? Who has shown up as a mentor,

guide, or teacher, and what did you learn from them? What gift did you discover because you met them?

- Where in your life have you made choices from a place of courage? From a place of confidence? From a place of defeat? Where did each of those choices lead you?
- As we all move towards the inevitable moment of death, how will you dance with life? What dreams are you igniting? How will you cultivate more joy and freedom?
- How do you know what you know, and how do you trust what you know? How does this knowing and trust in this knowing bolster the courage and confidence you need to keep walking your spiral path?

Of course, if you'd like to go beyond these questions and receive additional guidance in creating a *Fierce Awakenings* circle, reach out to any of the authors. As we mentioned in the introduction, we're walking with you on life's always changing and everlasting spiral path, and would love to accompany you to your next mile marker.

Cheers to all of us! Onwards and upwards we all go!

THANK YOU!

Dear Reader,

Your joyful presence has meant the world to us!

A million thank yous for trusting your intuition and following whatever cosmic breadcrumbs led you here, to our book.

We hope it filled your fierceness cup. We hope you'll use our stories and worksheets as a source to replenish your courage and confidence when you encounter the friction that keeps life interesting and the spiral path rewarding. We hope our paths will intersect in many more ways, and that we'll walk together onwards, inwards, and upwards.

We invite you to stay in touch with us in whatever way feels good to you. Click through the links in our bios to discover new ways to connect. So many things are unfolding beyond this book, and we would love for you to be part of the exciting journey being mapped alongside new dreams.

If you have found this book to be nurturing, inspiring, useful and/or satisfying to read, please take a minute to leave an honest review on Amazon **amzn.to/3EmdrUM** and/or **Goodreads.com.**

If you know someone who would benefit from this book, consider gifting them a copy. It's in the sharing that we all learn, that we all rise, and that we all shine.

RED THREAD PUBLISHING

Red Thread Publishing is an all-female publishing company on a mission to support 10,000 women to become successful published authors and thought leaders. Through the transformative work of writing and telling our stories we are not only changed as individuals, but we are also changing the global narrative & thus the world.

www.redthreadbooks.com

See our catalog of books:
    bit.ly/RedThreadLibrary

facebook.com/redthreadpublishing

instagram.com/redthreadbooks

Made in the USA
Las Vegas, NV
23 September 2023

77986665R00104